SCOTNOT
Number

C000084818

Robert Burns

by

Kenneth Simpson

Association for Scottish Literary Studies 1994

Published by
Association for Scottish Literary Studies
c/o Department of Scottish History
9 University Gardens
University of Glasgow
Glasgow G12 8QH

www.asls.org.uk

First published 1994
Reprinted 1997, 2000, 2001, 2004, 2007

A CIP catalogue for this title is available from the British Library

ISBN 978 0 948877 22 3

The Association for Scottish Literary Studies
is in receipt of subsidy from the Scottish Arts Council

Typeset by Roger Booth Associates, Hassocks, West Sussex
Printed by Ritchie (UK) Ltd, Kilmarnock

CONTENTS

EDITORS' FOREWORD

The *Scotnotes* booklets are a series of study guides to major Scottish writers and literary texts that are likely to be elements within literature courses. They are aimed at senior pupils in secondary schools and students in further education colleges and colleges of education. Each booklet in the series is written by a person who is not only an authority on the particular writer or text but also experienced in teaching at the relevant levels in schools or colleges. Furthermore, the editorial board, composed of members of the Schools and Further Education Committee of the Association for Scottish Literary Studies, considers the suitability of each booklet for the students in question.

For many years there has been a shortage of readily accessible critical notes for the general student of Scottish literature. *Scotnotes* has grown as a series to meet this need, and provides students with valuable aids to the understanding and appreciation of the key writers and major texts within the Scottish literary tradition.

Lorna Borrowman Smith
Ronald Renton

TEXTUAL NOTE

The edition used is *Poems and Songs of Robert Burns,* edited and introduced by James Barke (London and Glasgow: Collins, first published 1955). Extracts from the letters are from *The Letters of Robert Burns,* edited J. De Lancey Ferguson: second edition, edited G. Ross Roy (Oxford: Clarendon Press, 1985).

ACKNOWLEDGEMENTS

I acknowledge with gratitude the expertise of Jean Fraser in the preparation of the manuscript, and the wise, kindly, and – above all – patient counsel of the Scotnotes Editorial Board and, in particular, Alan MacGillivray, Jan Mathieson, Lorna Borrowman Smith and Ronald Renton.

The scholarship of Thomas Crawford, David Daiches, Donald Low, Carol McGuirk and G. Ross Roy has proved invaluable. The onus for errors lies solely with the author.

MYTH AND POET

For two centuries the poetry of Robert Burns (1759–1796) has enjoyed widespread popularity; and deservedly so, for Burns is a fine poet. However the price of that popularity is the myth that has come to surround Burns, as a result of which he has been reduced far too readily to a set of stereotypes. This process may reflect a Scottish need to create a national icon. A figurehead representative of allegedly Scottish characteristics serves as a focus for national pride and functions as a compensation for loss of nationhood. For those who would adhere to the myth a poem such as 'To John Kennedy, Dumfries House' represents the essence of Burns – love of the lasses (stanza 1); liquor – enough, but not to excess (stanzas 2–3); dislike of snobbery (stanza 4); and recognition of the importance of the feeling heart (stanza 5). While each of these qualities reflects an aspect of Burns, there is much more to both the man and the poet than that. The myth reduces Burns to manageable proportions and ignores the complexity of the man and the rich diversity of the poetry. It presents a partial, and hence distorted, Burns.

By taking an equally selective approach it would be possible on the evidence of some of the poems and letters to create another Burns, the complete antithesis to the apostle of the brotherhood of mankind who is toasted annually around the world. It was also Burns who wrote,

> I love to see a man who has a mind superior to the world and the world's men – a man who, conscious of his own integrity, and at peace with himself, despises the censures and opinions of the unthinking rabble of mankind. The distinction of a poor man and a rich man is something indeed, but it is nothing to the difference between either a wise man and a fool, or a man of honor and a knave.[1]

This does not sound like the Burns of the myth. Neither does this:

> However respectable Individuals in all ages have been, I have ever looked on Mankind in the lump to be nothing better than a foolish, headstrong, credulous, unthinking Mob; and their universal belief has ever had extremely little weight with me (*Letters*, I, 349).

I cite such statements not out of a desire to create an elitist Burns nor in a spirit of iconoclasm. The point is that the elitist Burns would be just as much a simplification and distortion of the truth as the Burns of myth is.

Burns is multi-faceted, both in respect of his complex personality and the many poetic modes and voices which he employs. Burns appears variously as ploughman-poet, Scotia's bard, sentimental Jacobite, loyal Unionist, rational observer of life, and man of feeling. The man who wrote some of the most tender of love lyrics was also a merciless satirist who used words as weapons, threatening the opponents of his friend, Dr. William McGill; 'I shall keep no measure with the savages, but fly at them with the faulcons of Ridicule, or run them down with the blood-hounds of Satire, as lawful game, wherever I start them' (*Letters*, I, 175). There was a Burns for whom Henry Mackenzie's *The Man of Feeling* (1771), the prime sentimentalist text, was the book prized 'next to the Bible' (*Letters*, I, 17); this was the Burns who, in 'To a Mountain Daisy', could feel compassion for a flower whose stem he had severed with his plough. There was also a Burns whose 'sarcastic humour' Mackenzie felt worthy of remark, a Burns who acknowledged his 'pride of stomach' (*Letters*, I, 17) and championed the cause of 'fair, candid ridicule' (*Letters*, II, 345). They were the same man and the same poet.

There is another enduring aspect of the myth which seems to fly in the face of the many-sided Burns which I have been proposing – the belief that Burns was a simple farmer miraculously blessed with poetic gifts, or, as Henry Mackenzie dubbed him, the 'Heaven-taught ploughman'. One aim of this introductory chapter is to offer an explanation of how this came to be, but for the moment it is important to recognise that Burns helped to perpetuate this image of himself. Here is part of the self-description with which he prefaced his Commonplace Book:

> Observations, Hints, Songs, Scraps of Poetry &c. by
> Robt Burness; a man who had little art in making
> money, and still less in keeping it; but was, however,
> a man of some sense, a great deal of honesty, and
> unbounded good-will to every creature rational or
> irrational. As he was but little indebted to scholastic
> education, and bred at a plough-tail, his performan-
> ces must be strongly tinctured with his unpolished,
> rustic way of life; but as I believe, they are really his
> own, it may be some entertainment to a curious

observer of human-nature to see how a ploughman thinks, and feels, under the pressure of Love, Ambition, Anxiety, Grief with the like cares and passions, which, however diversified by the Modes and Manners of life, operate pretty much alike I believe, in all the Species.[2]

That word 'performance' is crucially important: many of Burns's poems were exactly that – performances in which he acts a part – and one of these was the part of the untutored rustic. In the above extract style and substance are totally at odds: in highly polished prose Burns claims that he is unpolished.

The truth of the matter is that Burns was a complex individual, and the diverse voices of his poems, songs, and letters testify to this. In the poem 'Inscribed to the Right Hon. C. J. Fox' Burns writes,

> How Wisdom and Folly meet, mix, and unite,
> How Virtue and Vice blend their black and their white,
> How Genius, th' illustrious father of fiction,
> Confounds rule and law, reconciles contradiction,
> I sing.

Recognising the enigma that is human nature, he continues,

> Good Lord, what is Man! For as simple he looks,
> Do but try to develop his hooks and his crooks!
> With his depths and his shallows, his good and his evil,
> All in all he's a problem must puzzle the Devil.

That essential complexity of human nature was something which Burns both recognised and exemplified. In his hands the verse-epistle became a medium for expressing the flux of his mind and all its attendant contradictions. Rightly, Thomas Crawford commented, 'The self-dramatisations of the epistles express a mind in motion, giving itself over at different times to *conflicting* principles and feelings; they mirror that mind as it grappled with a complex world'.[3] Burns's mind ranges widely and freely in the various epistles to Lapraik, William Simpson, John Rankine, and John Goldie. In 'Epistle to James Smith', contrasting himself with those who 'with steady aim, some Fortune chase', he offers a description which might be taken as a metaphor for his progress in the epistle itself:

And others like your humble servan',
Poor wights! nae rules nor roads observin,
To right or left eternal swervin,
        They zig-zag on;
Till, curst with age, obscure an' starvin,
        They aften groan.

In 'A Poet's Welcome to his Love-begotten Daughter' (also entitled 'Welcome to a Bastart Wean') Burns conveys the mixture of emotions which the event – the birth of his daughter, Elizabeth, to Bess Paton, a family servant – has prompted in him. The first note is one of affectionate pride:

Thou's welcome, wean! Mishanter fa' me,
If thoughts o' thee or yet thy mammie
Shall ever daunton me or awe me,
        My sweet, wee lady,
Or if I blush when thou shalt ca' me
        Tyta or daddie!

However, this gives way almost immediately to a note of defensiveness and a defiance of convention:

What tho' they ca' me fornicator,
An' tease my name in kintra clatter?
The mair they talk, I'm kend the better;
        E'en let them clash!
An auld wife's tongue's a feckless matter
        To gie ane fash.

In the stanzas which follow the note alternates between loving concern for his daughter and pride in her, and these notes are united in the final stanza:

And if thou be what I wad hae thee,
An' tak the counsel I shall gie thee,
I'll never rue my trouble wi' thee –
        The cost nor shame o't –
But be a loving father to thee,
        And brag the name o't.

In this poem Burns communicates very clearly the mixed emotions which he feels.

Not all of Burns's poems are as directly personal; in few are his own feelings exposed quite so obviously. Rather, many of his poems are the result of his projecting his views or experiences on to a persona, a speaking voice or narrator. In such poems Burns has succeeded in finding a means of rendering his views, rather than stating them directly. On a number of occasions Burns indicates that he is aware of the way in which rhetoric may be used as a means of distancing himself from the experience. There are even some points when he sees it as a refuge or a means of concealing the true self. In 'Epistle to a Young Friend', a poem underpinned by a keen sense of the human enigma, this advice is offered:

> Conceal yoursel as weel's ye can
> Frae critical dissection:
> But keek thro' ev'ry other man
> Wi' sharpen'd, sly inspection.

Burns was essentially a chameleon. Personally charismatic, he was in both his writing and his social life adept at role-playing and a master in the creation of voices. Maria Riddell is testimony to this with her comment, 'none certainly ever outshone Burns in the charms – the sorcery, I would almost call it, of fascinating conversation, the spontaneous eloquence of social argument, or the unstudied poignancy of brilliant repartee'.[4] 'Sorcery' is a key term. In effect, that is what Burns was, a magician with words, and that ability informed both his writing and his social life.

To make such a claim is not in any way to question Burns's integrity as a poet; quite the reverse, since what he is doing is exploiting all the resources of language and literary techniques at his disposal in an attempt to render varieties of experience, both real and imagined. Burns's immense expressive energy, that sorcery with words, is channelled through a wide range of literary forms to an extent that reveals him as a sophisticated literary artist of the highest order, not a ploughman who happened to be blessed with divine inspiration.

The richness and diversity of Burns's writing may be traced in part to the literary and cultural influences upon him. In childhood he heard many old Scots songs from his mother, and from Betty Davidson, a relative who lived with the family, he had access to the native oral tradition. Burns wrote of her,

> She had, I suppose, the largest collection in the county of tales and songs concerning devils, ghosts, fairies, brownies, witches, warlocks, spunkies, kelpies, elf-candles, dead-lights, wraiths, apparitions, cantraips, giants, inchanted towers, dragons and other trumpery. – This cultivated the latent seeds of Poesy (*Letters*, I, 135).

William Burnes, Robert's father, was determined that his sons should have as much formal education as the demands of the farm would allow, and so, with some neighbouring families, he hired John Murdoch as teacher. Murdoch's main text-book, Arthur Masson's *Collection of Prose and Verse*, offered the young Burns a selection from the works of such writers as Shakespeare, Milton, Dryden, Addison, Gray and Shenstone. The important point is that Masson confined his selection to English authors; no Scottish material was included. If Burns's formal education was sporadic it was nonetheless very effective, aided as it was by his powers of absorption and his gift of mimicry. At a very early stage the seeds of his biculturalism were sown: at home he heard tales and songs of the supernatural, in the classroom he confronted the measured Augustan rationalism of Alexander Pope. His acute memory was to ensure that these disparate influences would later make their mark on his poetry.

A further influence, and a strong one, was the example set by Allan Ramsay (1684–1758) and Robert Fergusson (1750–1774) in reviving in the eighteenth century the tradition of vernacular Scots poetry. After the Union of the Parliaments in 1707 there was concern in Scotland that the nation's distinct cultural and literary traditions would not survive. Conscious of the need to preserve the Scottish poetic tradition, Ramsay published in 1724 *The Ever Green*, a collection of some of the poems of the Makars, late-medieval Scottish poets, the foremost of whom were William Dunbar, Robert Henryson, and Gavin Douglas; and in *The Tea-Table Miscellany* Ramsay offered a selection of songs in both Scots and English. In their poetry both Ramsay and Fergusson breathed new life into the techniques of the older, native tradition. Following the example of Dunbar and Henryson, Ramsay and Fergusson made effective use of the contrast between formal English and vernacular Scots. Such juxtaposition in terms of language was an ideal means of contrasting illusion and reality, or pretension and fact, and it was particularly useful to a social satirist as a means of undermining hypocrisy, formality, or vanity. As we will see, Burns's expressive Scots vernacular is instrumental in the unmasking of all that he regards as false.

In Ramsay and Fergusson Burns also found the distinctive stanza-form which he was to use for a wide range of expressive purposes. The stanza-form came to be known as 'Standard Habbie'. Ramsay had found it used in the poem, 'The Life and Death of Habbie Simpson, the Piper of Kilbarchan', by Robert Sempill of Beltrees (*c.*1595–*c.*1659). In his first 'Answer' to

William Hamilton of Gilbertfield, with whom he was exchanging
verse-epistles, Ramsay both used the stanza and gave it its name:

> May I be licket wi' a bittle
> Gin of your numbers I think little;
> Ye're never rugget, shan, nor kittle,
>   But blyth and gabby,
> And hit the spirit to a tittle,
>   Of Standart *Habby*.

With this particular stanza-form the rise and fall of the lines is
particularly effective in conveying movement of thought. Typically
a stage in the thought is reached by the fourth line, only to be
either clinched or undermined in lines five and six. Burns's
versatility with this stanza was remarkable: he used it in elegies,
epistles, and addresses for both comic and serious purposes.

There is one other striking feature of the Scottish poetic
tradition from the Makars to Ramsay and Fergusson which is
typified in the work of Burns: it is the momentum and verve of the
language, the sense in which the poet seems to relish the
expressive energy of language for its own sake. It is the sheer joy
in words, the joy of making which so characterises the Makars.
Precisely this spirit informs Burns's 'Address to the Toothache':

> My curse upon your venom'd stang,
> That shoots my tortur'd gooms alang,
> An' thro' my lug gies monie a twang
>   Wi' gnawing vengeance,
> Tearing my nerves wi' bitter pang,
>   Like racking engines!
>
> A' down my beard the slavers trickle,
> I throw the wee stools o'er the mickle,
> While round the fire the giglets keckle
>   To see me loup,
> An', raving mad, I wish a heckle
>   Were i' their doup!
>
> When fevers burn, or ague freezes,
> Rheumatics gnaw, or colic squeezes,
> Our neebors sympathise to ease us
>   Wi' pitying moan;
> But thee! – thou hell o' a' diseases,
>   They mock our groan!

Of a' the num'rous human dools –
Ill-hairsts, daft bargains, cutty-stools,
Or worthy frien's laid i' the mools,
            Sad sight to see!
The tricks o' knaves, or fash o' fools –
            Thou bear'st the gree!

Whare'er that place be priests ca' Hell,
Whare a' the tones o' misery yell,
An' ranked plagues their numbers tell
            In dreadfu' raw,
Thou, Toothache, surely bear'st the bell
            Amang them a'!

O thou grim, mischief-making chiel,
That gars the notes o' discord squeel,
Till humankind aft dance a reel
            In gore a shoe-thick,
Gie a' the faes o' Scotland's weal
            A towmond's toothache.

Language is functioning here as both therapy and sport (witness
the rhyme 'shoe-thick/toothache'). The rhythms of the Standard
Habbie stanza and the vernacular terms (in particular the rhymes
in stanzas one, two, and four) combine to great humorous effect.
The origins of this vigorously expressive and frequently abusive
manner are in the flyting mode. Burns is exploiting all his
resources of sound, sense, and rhythm to flyte the toothache.
    Flyting is both a poetic technique and, particularly in Scotland,
a social phenomenon. Essentially it is a contest in insult or
vilification. For the entertainment of the Stuart court, poets would
engage in a duel with words, directing all their resources of
language to the sole purpose of demeaning their opponents.
Likewise, mutual haranguing, especially between women, was a
traditional feature of Scottish street-life. Though found in various
European cultures, flyting seems to have particularly thrived in
Scotland, and it endured long after the demise of the late-medieval
culture in which it developed. In 'The Brigs of Ayr' Burns's bridges
flyte one another; in 'Address to a Haggis' Burns's speaker flytes
both continental cuisine and those reared on it; and in 'Tam
o' Shanter' the narrator reproduces the terms in which Tam's
nagging wife, Kate, has flyted him. Amongst the descendants of
flyting are the Glaswegian 'sherracking' or 'shirracking', of which
there are examples in *No Mean City*, by Alexander McArthur and
H. Kingsley Long, and in Edwin Morgan's poem, 'King Billy'. Why

has this phenomenon so endured in Scotland? Perhaps the answer is that the Scot, failing to find an outlet for intellect and energy, redirects that energy into the sheer momentum of language itself; if, particularly since the Union, Scots have had a sense of being unable to focus upon an ideal or channel their energies into the shaping of their lives – and Calvinist predetermination is far from blameless here either – then there is at least the alternative gesture of words. To the descendants of the flyting tradition we might add Rab C. Nesbitt's railings against the world. Likewise, with Burns, language functions as therapy and sport, but also, in a very real sense, as compensation.

This sense, so frequent in Scottish life and letters, of energy seeking – often in vain – for a focus or outlet alerts us to the broader issue of the Scottish quest for identity, a quest in which, as we noted at the outset, Burns has come to play a representative role for many Scots. There is abundant evidence to indicate that after the Union of 1707 Scots experienced a crisis of national identity. It was partly exacerbated by, and it is certainly reflected in, the language duality. Educated Scots were determined that Scotland should play its part culturally within the Union. But the crucial choice facing Scottish writers was one of language: should they remain true to the native vernacular tradition, and in so doing limit their range of readership, or should they reach the widest possible readership by using standard English but pay the price with a sense of guilt at abandoning their native culture? Burns was fluent in both vernacular Scots and formal English, a point which can be substantiated by comparing 'Tam o' Shanter' with Burns's prose account of the same material in a letter to the English antiquary, Captain Francis Grose (*Letters*, II, 29–31). It is by modulating the two languages that Burns achieves some of his most expressive effects. However from his first visit to Edinburgh in November 1786 he was under increasing pressure from the *literati* to write in English and avoid Scotticisms. This may explain his turning more and more in the last six years of his life to writing and collecting songs, though, ironically, even here he was encouraged to anglicise.

This tension in terms of language was a clear symptom of the Scottish problem of identity in the eighteenth century. In his *Journal of a Tour to the Hebrides* (1775) the Englishman, Dr. Samuel Johnson, had observed that 'languages are the pedigree of nations'. His Scottish fellow-traveller, James Boswell, had previously identified the problem facing the Scots. Boswell noted that since 'books and public discourse in Scotland are in the

English tongue...although an Englishman often does not understand a Scot, it is rare that a Scot has trouble in understanding
what an Englishman says'. Whereas for Scots the ideal might
have been dual nationality with its attendant advantages, the
reality was a kind of limbo characterised by an awareness of a
lack of wholeness of identity. To understand readily, but to have to
work at being understood, prompted self-consciousness and an
element of the schizoid.

The problem of Scottish identity was to be solved, but only
temporarily and in such a way as to leave the mark of sentimen-
tality on the Scottish personality and some of its literature. The
problem was solved by an accident of history, a coincidence of
circumstances. The middle of the eighteenth century witnessed a
growing challenge to one of the central tenets of the European
Enlightenment – the belief that by exercising his rational powers
man might steadily improve the human condition. Increasing
industrialisation and urbanisation seemed to call this promise
into question. William Blake was to write of 'dark, Satanic mills'
and a visit to Carron Ironworks was to draw this response from
Burns:

> We cam na here to view your warks
>   In hopes to be mair wise,
> But only, lest we gang to Hell,
>   It may be nae surprise.
> But when we tirl'd at your door
>   Your porter dought na bear us:
> Sae may, should we to Hell's yetts come,
>   Your billie Satan sair us.
>   ('At Carron Ironworks')

Industrialisation seemed to make a mockery of the desire for
human improvement. If Reason had so failed, man must seek
salvation from a different quarter. Thus the reaction against
Reason was epitomised in Rousseau's advocacy of a return to the
natural condition of our ancestors, that of an open and benign
emotionalism. Reason must give way to the values of the feeling
heart. 'Back to Nature' was the cry.

So began the quest to find the people who resembled most
closely our ancestor, the Noble Savage. The fate of Jacobite
Rebellion seemed to exemplify the sacrifice of an ancient and
noble culture on the altar of the destructive forces of rationalist
civilisation. Thus the Scottish Highlander joined the native
American as prime contenders for the title of descendant of the

Noble Savage. Here for the Scots was a solution to the problem of identity. The mantle of open emotionalism and natural benevolence fell upon the Scot and he seized it eagerly: here was an identity which gave him pre-eminence on the European stage; and at the same time Scotland's right to cultural partnership in the Union must surely be legitimised.

All that remained was to find the Noble Savage as poet. Enter Burns, to be feted by the overjoyed Edinburgh *literati*. To modern eyes it may seem rather odd that Burns's speaker in 'To a Mountain Daisy' should address with such tenderness a little flower whose stem he had just severed with his plough. In the context of the return to Nature and the values of sensibility such an attitude becomes more comprehensible. Burns wrote of the poem, 'I am a good deal pleased with some sentiments in it myself; as they are just the native, querulous feelings of a heart, which, as the elegantly melting Gray says, "Melancholy has marked for her own"' (*Letters*, I, 32); and Henry Mackenzie praised it for illustrating 'the tender and the moral'. What heaven teaches is natural benevolence; heaven's greatest gift is the values of the heart.

Burns genuinely endorsed the values of the heart, as his poems and songs testify. For instance, here is the conclusion of 'Address to the Unco Guid':

> Who made the heart, 'tis He alone
>   Decidedly can try us:
> He knows each chord, its various tone,
>   Each spring, its various bias:
> Then at the balance let's be mute,
>   We never can adjust it;
> What's done we partly may compute,
>   But know not what's resisted.

As a believer in the values of the heart, Burns could, in *this* respect, lay claim to the title of 'Heaven-taught ploughman'. But in playing the part he had to pretend to be divinely inspired. Recruited to the cause of establishing Scottish pre-eminence in the vogues of noble savagery and sensibility, and not unwilling to play the part, Burns then had to masquerade as the unpolished peasant who got inspiration from on high. Thus a complex personality and a widely read and sophisticated writer was reduced to fit the image of the peasant poet. However, the constraints affected the personality and the reputation rather than the poetry itself.

POET AND COMMUNITY

What was Burns's relationship to the rural community in which he lived and worked? Certainly his experience of life in such a community was invaluable to him as a poet. Burns was adept at observing and rendering the social energies of communal life, as this extract from 'The Holy Fair' demonstrates:

> Here farmers gash, in ridin graith,
> > Gaed hoddin by their cotters;
> There swankies young, in braw braid-claith,
> > Are springin owre the gutters.
> The lasses, skelpin barefit, thrang,
> > In silks an' scarlets glitter;
> Wi' sweet-milk cheese, in monie a whang,
> > An' farls, bak'd wi' butter,
> > > Fu' crump that day.

This description typifies a tradition in Scottish poetry of dynamic depiction of communal life, a tradition that stretches back via Fergusson and Ramsay to Dunbar. As a farmer, Burns was a participant in such activities, but with his keen eye and alert ear he was forever observing. What he habitually represents is a society whose experience is largely communal; and in many of Burns's poems there is a strong sense of fellowship, both among human beings and between them and the natural world. In the first 'Epistle to J. Lapraik' it is his awareness of the activities in the natural world that prompts the poet to go on to celebrate the socialising among human beings:

> While briers an' woodbines budding green,
> And paitricks scraichin loud at e'en,
> An' morning poussie whiddin seen,
> > Inspire my Muse,
> This freedom, in an unknown frien'
> > I pray excuse.
>
> On Fasten-e'en we had a rockin,
> To ca' the crack and weave our stockin;
> And there was muckle fun and jokin
> > Ye need na doubt;
> At length we had a hearty yokin,
> > At 'sang about'.

However it is important to note that Burns does not merely record rural life. Generally he brings his imagination to play upon his experiences. For example, Burns had a friend, Thomas Samson, who was an enthusiastic hunter and sportsman. On one occasion Samson remarked that he wanted to be buried on the moors over which he so regularly hunted. Taking this as his cue, Burns composed the mock-elegy, 'Tam Samson's Elegy'. Burns celebrates Samson's sporting prowess (stanza 5, for instance, gives a brief but vivid account of his skill at curling), but, ingeniously inverting the tradition of elegy whereby the natural world shares in the mourning, he depicts the lucky escape of those creatures which would have been Samson's next prey:

> Now safe the stately sawmont sail,
> And trouts bedropp'd wi' crimson hail,
> And eels, weel-kend for souple tail,
>   And geds for greed,
> Since, dark in Death's fish-creel, we wail,
>   Tam Samson dead!
>
> Rejoice, ye birring paitricks a';
> Ye cootie moorcocks, crousely craw;
> Ye maukins, cock your fud fu' braw
>   Withouten dread;
> Your mortal fae is now awa:
>   Tam Samson's dead!

Increasingly, however, the voice of the detached observer begins to vie with that of enthusiastic participant for pride of place in both Burns's poems and his letters. In 'The Vision', for instance, Burns presents the poet as the observer of the life of the community and thus someone set apart by virtue of that very fact. In an early letter (15 January 1783) Burns wrote to John Murdoch, 'the joy of my heart is to "Study men, their manners, and their ways"' (*Letters*, I, 17; the line is quoted from Pope's 'January and May'). Of necessity, the observer cannot also be the participant.

This process of distancing the poet from his community was accelerated by Burns's talent as satirist. From his fellow-poet, David Sillar, comes this account of the ambivalent response which Burns's ability as satirist induced:

> Mr. Robert Burns was sometime in the parish of
> Tarbolton prior to my acquaintance with him. His
> social disposition easily procured him acquaintance;
> but a certain satirical seasoning, with which he and

> all poetical geniuses are in some degree influenced, while it set the rustic circle in a roar, was not unaccompanied by its kindred attendant – suspicious fear. I recollect hearing his neighbours observe he had a great deal to say for himself, and that they suspected his *principles*. He wore the only tied hair in the parish; and in the church, his plaid, which was of a particular colour, I think *fillemot*, he wrapped in a particular manner around his shoulders.[5]

This suggests that Burns recognised that his abilities as poet made him a distinctive figure in the community; and plainly his dress and appearance further contributed to the identity which his talent and activities had created for him. As Sillar's testimony implies, Burns's situation was paradoxical. Burns was a sociable individual and he was, by all accounts, very entertaining company. But for his contemporaries, appreciation of his talent was accompanied by 'suspicious fear' that one might be his next victim. Equally, the 'satirical seasoning' was likely to get the poet himself into scrapes. Maria Riddell observed that 'the keenness of [Burns's] satire' proved to be 'a dangerous talent', adding that 'his wit ... had always the start of his judgment' (Low (ed.), *Burns: Critical Heritage*, p.103).

A poem which exemplifies Burns's ability to satirise effectively from the basis of local experience is 'Address to the Unco Guid'. The Biblical epigraph asserts that all human beings are a mixture of good and evil, wisdom and folly, and it points to Burns's concern in the poem – to question man's right to pass judgement on his fellow-man. This was an issue which greatly occupied Burns. An entry for March 1784 in his First Commonplace Book reads,

> I have often observed ... that every man even the worst, have something good about them ... Let any of the strictest character for regularity of conduct among us, examine impartially how many of his virtues are owing to constitution and education; how many vices he has never been guilty of, not from any care or vigilance, but from want of opportunity...how much he is indebted to the World's good opinion, because the World does not know all; I say any man who can thus think, will scan the failings, nay the faults and crimes of mankind around him, with a brother's eye (cited Kinsley, *Poems and Songs*, III, 1030).

Burns's target in the poem is those who would censure others, rather than understand, i.e. the 'unco guid' with their holier-than-thou attitude. In the first stanza he depicts the complacency with which they assure themselves of their own piety and run their lives. The tone changes in stanza 2 as he addresses them with feigned reverence – 'ye venerable core' – and then sets himself up as counsel for the defence of the 'poor mortals' who choose 'glaikit Folly's portals'. The affectionate tone of the vernacular, contrasting with the cold formality of the English in this stanza, indicates that Burns's sympathies lie with the accused rather than the judges. In the third stanza he invites the 'unco guid' to consider what justification there is for their sense of superiority. He answers for them: the only difference is that they are better at concealing their failings. The sham nature of their pride is reflected in the contrast between the formal diction of lines 3–6 and the colloquial and vernacular terms (lines 7–8) which undermine it.

Stanzas 4–6 demonstrate admirably Burns's skill in the use of language as an index to values. Inflated language mimics the inflated sense of their own status on the part of the 'rigidly righteous'; colloquialism or vernacular Scots renders the realistic viewpoint from which it is observed and by which it is undermined. Burns excels in such modulation of language for reductive effect. 'Think, when your castigated pulse' – and then the formality is undermined – 'Gies now and then a wallop' (with the familiar 'gies' and the comic-sounding 'wallop' destroying any remnants of pretension). Similarly, the personified 'Social-life and Glee' become 'Debauchery and Drinking' courtesy of the comically Scotticised form, 'transmugrify'd', of the pompous, Latinate term. In stanza 6 formal address – 'Ye high, exalted, virtuous dames,/ Tied up in godly laces' – leads to the warning,

> Before ye gie poor Frailty names,
> Suppose a change o' cases:
> A dear-lov'd lad, convenience snug,
> A treach'rous inclination –

But then, having posited this possibility, the speaker rules it out: 'But, let me whisper i' your lug,/Ye're aiblins nae temptation'. The control of tone is masterly, the first line exuding confidentiality and concern, and the second demolishing everything with the brutal truth.

Having shown that the 'unco guid' exemplify the very fallibility which they are so ready to censure in others, the speaker then

makes a plea for humane understanding, rather than condemnation of human weakness (with the internal rhymes 'scan/man'
and 'gang/wrang' contributing to the gentle, almost compassionate
tone). The poem is essentially about the conflict between, on the
one hand, social order and codes of behaviour and, on the other,
individual instinct and impulse. Burns is implying that if that
conflict is enacted within the macrocosm of society it is also
present within the microcosm of the individual (even the 'high,
exalted virtuous dames' have needs which they would satisfy if a
sufficiently private opportunity presented itself). If the human
condition is one of internal conflict then instinct will inevitably
evade the control of judgement, action will out-run understanding.
That being so, compassionate understanding of human limitation,
not condemnation, is what is required. The ultimate point of the
poem is to endorse feeling and instinct as natural; in contrast,
judgement is the natural right, not of man, but of God who 'made
the heart'. From the basis of the specific address to the 'unco guid'
Burns has shaped a general truth: given that human nature will
defy both constraint and comprehension, the valid morality is that
of natural sympathy, not moral judgement.

Here Burns plainly writes as a satirist motivated by a concern
for his fellow-beings. The satirist is in an essentially ambivalent
situation: he is both within society, experiencing its injustices, and
on the margins of society, expressing his concern. As a medium,
satire is replete with paradox: if satire were truly effective it would
make itself redundant; there is, too, a risk of the satirist's
'preaching to the converted', with the target of the satire remain-
ing oblivious to its import; and, above all, there is the danger of
the satirist's becoming marginalised simply by virtue of his
function. One senses this in the case of Burns – that the satirist's
social concern involves him in devising satiric stratagems, which
in turn necessarily distances him from his community.

The satirist is both of the people and different. So it was with
Burns; and he seems to have recognised the fact. In the prefatory
note to the First Commonplace Book he wrote, '…I was placed by
Fortune among a class of men to whom my ideas would have been
nonsense'. Yet he also affirmed, '…my first ambition was, and still
my strongest wish is, to please my Compeers, the rustic Inmates
of the Hamlet' (*Letters*, I, 88), though his language here reflects
the fact that it is not to one of the 'rustic inmates' that he is
writing but rather to the London-based Scottish doctor and writer,
John Moore. Such terms in themselves suggest a measure of
distancing.

One of Burns's most remarkable achievements is to have written so many poems which operate meaningfully on at least two levels. In 'The Auld Farmer's New-Year Morning Salutation to his Auld Mare, Maggie', he creates a voice which would be authentic for many of his 'compeers', that of the elderly farmer looking back on a life of toil. Significantly, the farmer does not think to question why his life has been so hard. The monologue credibly represents the farmer's viewpoint but, courtesy of it, Burns is making a plea that enlightenment and improvement, if they are to be meaningful, must touch the lives of such ordinary people.

Burns is ingenious in devising means of incorporating his own breadth and depth of knowledge within what are apparently accounts of rural life. 'The Death and Dying Words of Poor Mailie' seems to owe its origin to animal fables and the 'last dying words' tradition. On one level the poem entertains as a humorous account of a rural commonplace – a sheep falling over and unable to get back on its feet. Much of the comedy derives from the ironic contrast between the dumb-struck human presence, Hughoc, and the lengthy and articulate address from the allegedly dying sheep. Through her account Mailie is characterised, and she is revealed as remarkably well read, being, as her message to her master indicates, conversant with Rousseau's advocacy of natural education:

> Tell him, if e'er again he keep
> As muckle gear as buy a sheep –
> O bid him never tie them mair,
> Wi' wicked strings o' hemp or hair!
> But ca' them out to park or hill,
> An' let them wander at their will.

She also possesses a sound sense of practical economics, which suggests she may be familiar with Adam Smith's *The Wealth of Nations*: 'So may his flock increase, an' grow/To scores o' lambs, an' packs o' woo'!'. The unfettered upbringing will be good for the sheep (no fear of tripping over the tether, like Mailie) and for the farmer (untethered sheep will breed more vigorously).

However, Mailie's dying wishes for her own children are somewhat at odds with the principle which she has been upholding. Here she expresses her concern that her son be brought up properly:

My poor toop-lamb, my son an' heir,
O, bid him breed him up wi' care!
An' if he live to be a beast,
To pit some havins in his breast!
An' warn him – what I winna name –
To stay content wi' yowes at hame;
An' no to rin an' wear his cloots,
Like other menseless, graceless brutes.

Far from running free, as Rousseau would advocate, he must avoid loose women and nights on the town. Likewise, her daughter is to steer clear of 'onie blastit, moorland toop' and mix only 'wi' sheep o' credit like thysel!'. The dying ewe is now genteel matron, concerned that her family should be a credit to her. Courtesy of a sheep as well-bred as well-read, Burns, ironically distanced, has highlighted the general human tendency to say one thing in theory and do quite another in practice. Rousseau's natural, unfettered education is admirable in theory, but it's the last thing Mailie would want for her own children; theories are for other people, not for ourselves. At the same time as entertaining the 'rustic inmates', Burns has found a means of accommodating some of his insight into human nature, and he has been able to bring his awareness of current intellectual trends to bear upon this. And all of this has been accomplished without his having to say anything in his own voice.

SATIRE AND SENTIMENT

Warmth, passion, and commitment were qualities which Burns regarded as essential to the poet. In one letter he referred to himself as possessing 'the bedlam warmth of a Poet's heart' (*Letters*, I, 155); in another he praised Gavin Hamilton's brother for having 'what with me is the Alpha and the Omega...a heart [that] might adorn the breast of a Poet' (*Letters*, I, 152). Warmth and passionate commitment inform both his love lyrics and his social satires.

These qualities were innate within Burns. However they also were endorsed in contemporary thought and particularly that of Scottish philosophers, most notably David Hume and Adam Smith, for whom the capacity to feel was an index to moral sense (the very title of Smith's *Theory of Moral Sentiments* making this plain). Burns was also to find the values of the heart featuring prominently in much of the imaginative literature to which he was drawn. Aged twenty-three, he wrote to John Murdoch, his former teacher,

> My favorite authors are of the sentimental kind, such as Shenstone, particularly his Elegies, Thomson, Man of feeling, a book I prize next to the Bible, Man of the World, Sterne, especially his Sentimental journey, Mcpherson's Ossian, etc. these are the glorious models after which I endeavour to form my conduct (*Letters*, I, 17).

The extent of the influence of sentimental literature upon him can be seen in the same letter where he projects the image of himself as 'the man whose mind glows with sentiments lighted up at their sacred flame – the man whose heart distends with benevolence to all the human race'; and then he resumes a more realistic awareness of his own situation, exclaiming, 'O how the glorious triumph swells my heart! I forget that I am a poor, insignificant devil'. The image of the man of feeling was an attractive one, though, and he was to employ it in his writing and, at times, in his behaviour.

In Henry Mackenzie's prose fiction, *The Man of Feeling* (1771), the values of the heart are promoted through the sensibility and the conduct of the eponymous hero, Harley, who relieves the suffering of a variety of unfortunates. Active benevolence is recommended not just for the advantage which it brings to the sufferer but also for the credit which it bestows on the benefactor, who takes satisfaction in contemplating himself in that role. In *The Man of Feeling* there is foregrounding of one of the central concepts of sentimental benevolence – 'self-approving joy'. The joy is two-fold: by sympathetic identification, the benefactor is able to share the victim's grief and so experiences, vicariously, the pleasures of melancholy; but, in his capacity of benefactor, he also has the satisfaction of both manifesting and contemplating his own open-heartedness.

The endorsement of sentiment in many of the texts which he read had significant implications for Burns: it validated his own natural warm-heartedness; it enabled him to create personae which, in epitomising benevolent sympathy, might serve – conveniently for the satirist – as contrasts to an otherwise cruel world; and it encouraged him to adopt some of the means whereby the capacity for feeling was given prominence.

Integral to the demand for a return to Nature was the belief that man's original state was one of natural feeling; furthermore, the contemplation of the natural world would induce natural feeling as a response. Add to this the habitual practice of the benefactor in the sentimental novel – to fix upon a wretched creature and address it in terms of compassionate sympathy – and we have the literary background upon which Burns was to draw in his Addresses 'To a Mouse', 'To a Louse', and 'To a Mountain Daisy'.

In 'To a Mouse' Burns immediately addresses the tiny creature, and he does so in a mixture of Scots-English and vernacular Scots:

> Wee, sleekit, cowrin, tim'rous beastie,
> O, what a panic's in thy breastie!
> Thou need na start awa sae hasty
>   Wi' bickering brattle!
> I wad be laith to rin an' chase thee,
>   Wi' murdering pattle!

The terms reveal the speaker's capacity for empathy: in two lines he has represented what it is to be that mouse – small, glossy, and terrified. At the start it is depicted as a threatened creature, but the speaker assures it that its normal reaction – to try to escape – is unnecessary in this case. This means that the speaker, too, is rapidly characterised: he is unusual in that not only has he taken time to address a mouse in terms which suggest he understands its condition but he is also disinclined to chase it. Thus the speaker is making a point of distancing himself from the 'normal' reaction of the majority. By addressing the mouse familiarly in terms of affectionate concern ('wee', 'cowrin', 'tim'rous', and the diminutives, 'beastie' and 'breastie') he is enlisting it in a community with himself. This is essential for the contrast which he draws in the next stanza:

> I'm truly sorry man's dominion
> Has broken Nature's social union,
> An' justifies that ill opinion
>   Which makes thee startle
> At me, thy poor, earth-born companion
>   An' fellow mortal!

Here the speaker appears to claim that there once existed a natural harmony between human beings and the creatures of the natural world. Regretting its demise, he sets about restoring it, at least in terms of relations between himself and the mouse. The formal English of stanza 2 conveys the essence of the speaker's philosophy, but he reverts to the vernacular to develop the specific example. The effect of using the familiar terms of the agricultural community, such as 'a daimen icker in a thrave', is to legitimise the mouse's membership of that community, a community in which the speaker can readily countenance its thieving in order to survive and in which he willingly spares it the left-over ear out of twenty-four sheaves, since he will be blest with the remainder and also, perhaps, with the knowledge that he has practised benevolence.

In stanzas 4–6 the speaker considers the plight of the mouse which, having built its nest as a protection against the onset of winter, now finds itself homeless. Again the speaker's terms have a familiarising effect and convey his affectionate concern: 'Thy wee-bit housie, too, in ruin!/Its silly wa's the win's are strewin!'. Burns's use of sound patterns to reinforce sense in stanzas 5 and 6 is especially effective: the hardships of oncoming winter ('Thou saw the fields laid bare an' waste,/An' weary winter coming fast') are reflected in the bleak sounds, and the remorseless movement of the seasons is emphasised by the alliteration of 'weary winter'. 'Cozie' conveys the expectation of comfort, which has now been dashed, just as the syntax is disrupted: 'Till crash! the cruel coulter past/Out thro' thy cell' (with the alliteration again implying irresistible force). Similarly in stanza 6 – 'That wee bit heap o' leaves an' stibble,/Has cost thee monie a wearie nibble!' – sound as well as sense suggests the prospect of limited but hard-won security, whereas the expressive use of harsh sounds ('But house

or hald,/To thole the winter's sleety dribble,/An' cranreuch cald')
reinforces the harshness of what lies ahead.

In empathising with the mouse in these stanzas the speaker
helps to repair the broken 'social union'. But it is noticeable that
he also endows the mouse with human characteristics. Why this
is being done becomes clear in stanza 7:

> But Mousie, thou art no thy lane,
> In proving foresight may be vain:
> The best-laid schemes o' mice an' men
> Gang aft agley,
> An' lea'e us nought but grief an' pain,
> For promis'd joy!

The effect of the speaker's both empathising with the mouse and
humanising it is to establish them as common victims of a cruel
world. Human and mouse alike fail to shape the course of their
lives and cannot bring plans to fruition. However in the final
stanza the humanised mouse reverts to being an ordinary mouse
to enable the speaker to contrast its blessing, in that it lives only
in the present, with his troubled recollection of past wretchedness
and fearful anticipation of an unknown future.

Of all Burns's poems it is 'To a Mouse' and 'Tam o' Shanter'
which are best known, and probably no lines of his are more often
cited than 'The best-laid schemes o' mice and men/Gang aft agley'
(which, with justification, David Daiches adduces as evidence of
'Burns's ability to cast a thought into the idiom of the folk
proverb').[6] Yet, looked at rationally, the poem is a tissue of
absurdities. The situation in itself is bizarre: in real life anyone
who declaimed at length to a mouse would be locked away, and
one wonders about a mouse which would hang around long
enough to be on the receiving end of a 48-line address. Burns's
speaker may well believe in 'Nature's social union', but Burns the
farmer would have no such naive illusions, knowing that the
created order is a hierarchy of predators and prey. Also, there
seems to be some inconsistency in the account of the mouse's
rational capacity: though capable of 'best-laid schemes' it is,
apparently, touched only by the present.

Yet the popular appeal of the poem would suggest that readers
are untroubled by such inconsistencies. This would confirm the
suspicion that the poem is a triumph of rhetoric, and it is a
triumph of a particular and very high order because the rhetoric,
completely disguised, goes unnoticed. Burns does not merely
present the persona of the benevolent sentimentalist: he uses it as

a means towards his end, which is to convey his satirist's concern for humanity. Courtesy of the identification of mouse and speaker as 'fellow mortals' and, more importantly, fellow-victims, Burns strikes a chord within the reader. His ultimate concern is to arouse our indignation at injustice, and he utilises some of the props of sentimentalist literature to that end. The means may derive from the vogue of sensibility but the end is the compassionate concern of satire.

Similarly, in 'To a Louse' Burns appears to be employing the stock-in-trade of sentimentalist literature in that, here again, the speaker addresses a small and insignificant creature. However, here too his concern is with satiric observation leading to a universal truth.

The direct address again lends dramatic immediacy: 'Ha! whare ye gaun, ye crowlin ferlie?', and the very sound of these words conveys the speaker's sense of outrage, which he deliberately exaggerates. Burns modulates tone in this poem to brilliant effect. Even in the first stanza itself the speaker moves from feigned indignation to feigned concern that the louse may derive little sustenance from its chosen hunting-ground. In the second stanza the speaker directs a torrent of abuse at the louse – 'Ye ugly, creepin, blastit wonner,/Detested, shunn'd by saunt an' sinner', a tirade typical of the flyting mode. The deliberate bluster of such terms is appropriate prelude to the speaker's exaggerated outburst of supposed horror at the louse's having the audacity to rise above its station and dine on a fine lady, rather than the lower classes as befits it. By this point Burns's satire on both artificial social hierarchies and the discrepancy between illusion and reality is well under way, the particularly telling irony being that it is an insignificant creature such as a louse which can transcend social barriers. That being the case, can those barriers have any real validity?

In the third stanza the speaker pretends to relegate the louse to his appropriate feeding-ground – the lower orders – and here the reductive effect of the sound conveys his feigned condescension: 'Swith! in some beggar's hauffet squattle:/There ye may creep, and sprawl, and sprattle'. But then the tone changes again as the speaker indulges in mock-heroic hyperbole:

> Wi' ither kindred, jumping cattle,
>> In shoals and nations:
> Where horn nor bane ne'er daur unsettle
>> Your thick plantations.

With his apparently callous disregard for the welfare of the
unfortunate beggar, home to 'shoals and nations' of lice, the
speaker is pretending once again to uphold the rigid social
hierarchy.

'To a Louse' is a vividly dramatic poem (in which respect – as
in other more obvious ways – it resembles Donne's 'The Flea'). The
fluctuations in tone mirror the speaker's changing responses to
the louse's movements. Stanza 4 brings another change of tone,
with the speaker advising the louse to stay hidden in the place of
safety which it has now reached. The implicit sexual metaphor is
maintained as the speaker exclaims at the louse's daring to
ascend to 'The vera tapmost, tow'ring height/O' Miss's bonnet'. In
stanza 5 the comic dimension to the speaker's response is evident
from the rhyming of 'nose out/grozet/rozet' and 'smeddum/
droddum', and also from the suggestion that he will counter great
offence with a comparably great threat. Reverting to his pose of
outrage, the speaker indicates that he would expect the louse to
know its place in the hierarchy. Here Burns subtly relates the
supposed vanity of the louse's aspirations to the actual vanity of
the young lady, resplendent in her Lunardi bonnet. This is a
particularly telling ironic detail. Vincenzo Lunardi, an Italian,
had instigated balloon-flights in London in 1784 and in Glasgow
and Edinburgh in the following year, and he delighted in being
known as 'the first aerial traveller in the English atmosphere'.
Ladies' hats in the shape of hot-air balloons rapidly became the
height of fashion. The reference to Lunardi evokes the louse's
comparably daring ascent, while both the young lady and the
Italian balloonist epitomise the folly of human vanity.

Both the speaker's focus and his tone change once again in
Stanza 7. Noticing that the louse has now reached the young
lady's face, he advises her, in a tone of affectionate, but also
amused, concern,

> O Jenny, dinna toss your head,
> An' set your beauties a' abread!
> Ye little ken what cursed speed
>   The blastie's makin!
> Thae winks an' finger-ends, I dread,
>   Are notice takin!

In trying to catch the louse she risks spoiling the beautiful effect
she has so proudly created, and already her efforts have attracted
the attention of those seated behind her and make her a comic
figure. These are his ostensible reasons for discouraging her, but

it might be suggested that, out of admiration for the louse's daring and persistence, he wants it to escape unscathed.

Of the last stanza Thomas Crawford has commented, 'The first four lines..., which extract a general truth from this concrete situation, have become proverbial throughout the English-speaking world, but perhaps because of their implicit criticism of sanctimoniousness the two concluding lines are seldom quoted:

> O wad some Power the giftie gie us
> To see oursels as ithers see us!
> It wad frae monie a blunder free us,
>   An' foolish notion:
> What airs in dress an' gait wad lea'e us
>   An' ev'n devotion!'
>   (Crawford, *Burns*, p.155)

The moral commentary develops naturally and justifiably out of the description of the incident. Those two last lines are vital as they embody the climactic irony. Just as the apparently insignificant louse is actually the free spirit which transcends all artificial barriers, so the last lines of the poem encompass all within their irony. It is Jenny who has exemplified 'airs in dress an' gait', but who is guilty of 'airs' in 'devotion'? Here it is worth remembering that the entire incident has taken place in church and has been witnessed and recorded in detail by the speaker during worship. This may suggest that there is little in the sermon to hold his attention (and certainly nothing to compete with the attractions of the young lady). Thus he sets himself up as a rival preacher and his address mimics the format of the sermon – anecdote/episode leading to universal truth (and the nature of his sermon conveniently enables him to study the beautiful young lady at length). The ultimate irony is that his alternative sermon is encompassed within the terms of the last line of the poem. There is one irony in Burns's using the lowly and traditionally insignificant louse to celebrate the triumph of classlessness. There is yet another, and even more subtle, irony in employing the apparent folly in the aspirations of the louse as the means of drawing together Jenny and the speaker (and probably also Lunardi) as human exemplars of the real folly, the folly of human vanity.

THE POET'S VOICES

Burns was a virtuoso in the creation of distinctive voices. In many of his poems he establishes a specific persona. This capacity would have served him well had he ever followed up his expressed intention of trying his hand at drama. Possibly he was prevented from doing so by a combination of the demands of his work, first as farmer and then as exciseman, and the general antipathy to drama in a society so dominated by Presbyterianism. As it was, the closest Burns was to come to drama was the cantata, 'The Jolly Beggars' (also entitled 'Love and Liberty').

Instead Burns's considerable dramatic talent found expression in his poems and also, to some extent, in his social life. In many of his poems Burns does not speak in his own voice but rather that of the distinct persona which he has created. He acknowledged, 'I cannot for the soul of me resist an impulse of any thing like Wit' (*Letters*, I, 392), and in following such impulses he often came to speak through personae. In poems such as 'Scotch Drink' and 'Address to a Haggis' he makes deliberately exaggerated claims in order to entertain; such bluster should not be equated with his own views on the subjects. In this context it is worth heeding the following comment from Burns's brother, Gilbert:

> ...every attentive reader of Burns's Works must have observed, that he frequently presents a caricature of his feelings, and even of his failings – a kind of mock-heroic account of himself and his opinions, which he never supposed could be taken literally (Low (ed.), *Burns: Critical Heritage*, p.271).

This point should be stressed, because some of his devotees are inclined to quote Burns as if he meant literally every line he wrote. To do so is to disregard his expertise in the use of poetic monologue. Browning is not synonymous with the speaker in 'My Last Duchess' nor T. S. Eliot with J. Alfred Prufrock. Likewise Burns is neither the 'Auld Farmer' or a dying sheep, but it says much that in the case of Burns the point has to be laboured, especially given that his letters testify to his recognition of the importance of the creative imagination. Asked to give his opinion of another poet's work, Burns offered this specific criticism:

I do not altogether like –
      – "Truth,
The soul of every song that's nobly great"–
Fiction is the soul of many a Song that's nobly great
                        (*Letters*, I, 326).

And he took pride in designating himself one of 'the harum-
scarum Sons of Imagination and Whim' (*Letters*, I, 109).

Such comments hint at another reason for Burns's creation of
so many different voices in his poetry. He does so not just as a
potential dramatist finding an alternative outlet for his dramatic
impulse but also as a highly intelligent inhabitant of a small
community. Burns exemplifies, in heightened form, one of the
paradoxes of Scottish life. The Reformation, blamed by Edwin
Muir for the alleged curtailment of Scottish culture, in fact
promoted popular education by the establishment of schools in
many parishes. Until well through the eighteenth century
Scotland comprised a mass of fairly small communities amongst
which there was little communication. Scots, then, were relatively
well educated but confined to a limiting environment (unless they
chose to leave their communities, as many did). If you live in a
village you soon come to know your neighbours' views on politics,
religion, and much else; and if your religion tells you that your
condition is given and cannot be changed, then there is much to be
said for using your imagination to create an alternative. Playing
devil's advocate offers an attractive outlet for intelligence as well
as enlivening the daily routine. So it was for Burns. Furthermore,
his adoption of a range of voices may be one individual's experience of the national crisis of identity (to which reference was
made earlier) and his attempt to express it and, hopefully, come to
terms with it. However, as will be indicated later, Burns's remarkable chameleon ability, which was productive of a wide range
of poems of the highest order, was to take its psychological toll of
the poet himself.

Religion is an appropriate starting-point for a consideration of
Burns's poetic use of voice and persona. Religion was one of the
earliest topics which prompted Burns to write poetry. In the first
of his ecclesiastical satires, 'The Twa Herds', Burns focuses on the
dispute between two Ayrshire preachers, 'Black Jock' Russell and
Alexander Moodie. Here Burns employs the tactic of having his
speaker offer the viewpoint to which he, Burns, is opposed – that
of the traditionalist faction in the Church of Scotland. In the
religious wrangles which so characterised Scottish life in the

eighteenth century the opposing parties were identified as 'Auld Lichts' and 'New Lichts'. The former were ultra-conservative and their doctrine, heavily reliant on literal interpretation of the Old Testament, foregrounded original sin and eternal damnation for all but those whom God had chosen for salvation, the Elect. In contrast, the New Lichts, with whose views Burns was much more in sympathy, offered a more humane and liberal reading of Scripture which gained further impetus from Scottish Enlightenment thought.

Nowhere does Burns convey more forcefully his own stance in this debate than in 'Holy Willie's Prayer'; and he does so without saying one word in his own voice. No poem demonstrates more convincingly Burns's facility in the creation of character, voice, and persona. Here the satiric use of voice, with which he had experimented in 'The Twa Herds', is brought to perfection. The technique is that of ironic self-revelation: the speaker, through his monologue, unwittingly reveals himself and his views and values in all their limitation. The poet remains detached throughout, ironically distanced from the character he has created. All unknowingly, the speaker is the means whereby the poet can communicate his views to the reader. There were precedents for this technique in Scottish poetry, most notably Allan Ramsay's 'Last Speech of a Wretched Miser', but Burns's achievement in the mode is supreme. It is not, of course, a feature exclusive to Scottish literature but its recurrence there (it is used to great effect by Hogg in both accounts in *Confessions of a Justified Sinner*, by Galt in *Annals of the Parish*, and by Stevenson in *Dr. Jekyll and Mr.Hyde*) suggests that it was a technique which particularly appealed to the Scottish penchant for satiric reduction, in which Scottish writers were especially adept. Undeniably, in 'Holy Willie's Prayer' the Scottish tradition of the ironic use of voice reaches its zenith.

As with many of Burns's finest poems, 'Holy Willie's Prayer' originated in very specific circumstances. In August 1784, Gavin Hamilton, a friend of Burns, had been charged at the annual communion at Mauchline with poor church attendance, making a journey on a Sunday, and writing an abusive letter to the kirk-session; it was further alleged that he had required some of his servants to work on the Sabbath. When the case was referred to them the presbytery of Ayr found in favour of Hamilton, to the particular annoyance of William Fisher, the elder who had been foremost in instigating the charges. Fisher was typical of those elders of the Auld Licht faction who took very seriously their duties as moral overseers of the behaviour of their parishioners.

Burns celebrates Hamilton's victory with what is allegedly the prayer offered by Holy Willie after his defeat. The epigraph, 'And send the godly in a pet to pray' (Pope, 'The Rape of the Lock', iv, 64) is thus highly appropriate. The poem assumes the formal sequence of the Presbyterian prayer: invocation and praise; confession and penitence; intercession and petition.

The first five stanzas give a clear indication of Holy Willie's creed. The opening line, resembling part of a psalm, gives no hint of what is to follow. This is quite deliberate to establish by contrast Holy Willie's worshipping of a whimsically authoritarian God:

> O Thou that in the Heavens does dwell,
> Wha, as it pleases best Thysel,
> Sends ane to Heaven an' ten to Hell
> A' for Thy glory,
> And no for onie guid or ill
> They've done before Thee!

The religious nature of the first line lulls the reader so that the doctrine of the following lines particularly shocks: what kind of God is this who assigns men to heaven or hell regardless of their conduct on earth, and what kind of religion is it which deals in terms of such fixed odds? The answer is immediately forthcoming:

> I bless and praise Thy matchless might,
> When thousands Thou hast left in night,
> That I am here before Thy sight,
> For gifts an' grace
> A burning and a shining light
> To a' this place.

Here, too, the first line is conventionally religious, whereas what follows reveals Holy Willie relishing the fact that he has been chosen for salvation. He is in no doubt that he is one of the Elect.

According to Calvinist doctrine God predetermines the ultimate fate of each individual. In Calvin's *Institutes*, III, xxi, 5 the doctrine is encapsulated:

> ...predestination we call the eternal decree of God by which He has determined with Himself what He would have so become of every man. For...eternal life is foreordained for some and eternal damnation for others. Every man...is predestinated to life or to death.

The true believer is assured of salvation even if at times that
assurance may seem to be called into question. Holy Willie, as a
true believer, is one of God's chosen. Thus, since he knows that he
is guaranteed salvation, he can risk asking why he has been so
favoured. His creed supplies the answer: it has been foreordained
by God. Thus what he is indulging in (stanzas 3–5) is really self-
congratulation. Willie's terminology here betrays his doctrine in
all its limitations: he accepts Bishop Ussher's dating of the
Creation and the Fall ('Sax thousand years ere my creation'), and
his depiction of the torments of hell reproduces, in terms whose
sound takes them close to parody,the essence of the hell-fire
sermon:

> When from my mither's womb I fell,
> Thou might hae plung'd me deep in hell
> To gnash my gooms, and weep, and wail
>   In burning lakes,
> Whare damned devils roar and yell,
>   Chain'd to their stakes.

Believing that he is saved, he spares no effort to render the
agonies, but all that he has at his disposal is the worst clichés of
the evangelicals. These serve also for his self-congratulation, and
diction, rhymes and rhythm convey his complacent certainty:

> Yet I am here, a chosen sample,
> To show Thy grace is great and ample:
> I'm here a pillar o' Thy temple,
>   Strong as a rock,
> A guide, a buckler, and example
>   To a' Thy flock!

This is highly ironic, given that, on a plane of which he is totally
unaware, he is being used as an 'example' by Burns.

Holy Willie's tone changes significantly as he turns from self-
congratulation to confession. 'Example' though he is, yet he is
sometimes 'fash'd wi' fleshly lust' – a phrase which typifies
Burns's practice throughout of mingling the idioms of the spoken
vernacular with the more formal language of the sermon. The
tone here is not, however, one of genuine humility. Guaranteed
eternal salvation, Holy Willie has no need to be humble; here he is
merely playing the part of the meek and fallible mortal. The same
may be said of stanza 7:

> O Lord! yestreen, Thou kens, wi' Meg –
> Thy pardon I sincerely beg –
> O, may't ne'er be a living plague
>   To my dishonour!
> An' I'll ne'er lift a lawless leg
>   Again upon her.

The faltering syntax of the first line does not convey shame or embarrassment or humility. As 'Thou kens' makes plain, Holy Willie has no need to confess. Just as his God 'kens' everything, so Holy Willie knows confession is irrelevant since his salvation is preordained. Here, too, he is simply playing the part of the penitent; but why, since God presumably 'kens' this too? Can it be that even God's chosen resorts to role-playing to enliven his given condition?

Emboldened by the certainty of his election, Holy Willie elaborates on his recent misdemeanours:

> Besides, I farther maun avow –
> Wi' Leezie's lass, three times, I trow –
> But, Lord, that Friday I was fou,
>   When I cam near her,
> Or else, Thou kens, Thy servant true
>   Wad never steer her.

The first two lines of this stanza come very close to bar-room boasting of sexual prowess, but this 'men's talk' is between a kirk elder and God. Recalling that he is the Lord's servant, Holy Willie then feels the need to explain his sins of fornication. How did it happen? – He was drunk. Rather than having the courage to admit that he succumbed to instinctive desires, he demeans himself, unwittingly, by his grovelling attempt at an excuse.

In stanzas 7 and 8 Burns makes particularly effective use of a technique which is in evidence throughout the poem. Such is Holy Willie's intimacy with his God that he can address him in terms which are an amalgam of the colloquial idioms of the rural community ('I'll ne'er lift a lawless leg/Again upon her', and 'wad never steer her') and the vocabulary of the Presbyterian evangelicals, known as 'the language of the saints' ('a living plague'; 'thy servant true'). In a sense Willie *is* his language; and his language reflects the terms of his existence, which are, jointly, those of 'Auld Licht' Presbyterianism and the parochial rural community. By addressing his Lord as a familiar in such limited terms, Willie reduces him to his level. The limitations of the creed are further emphasised by the localising of its God within the parish.

After his 'confession' Holy Willie speculates as to why God allows him to sin:

> Maybe Thou lets this fleshly thorn
> Buffet Thy servant e'en and morn,
> Lest he owre proud and high should turn
>   That he's sae gifted:
> If sae, Thy han' maun e'en be borne
>   Until Thou lift it.

'Fleshly lust' has become 'fleshly thorn'. What may seem to be humility here is soon revealed as self-righteousness relishing its own devious logic. Holy Willie asks God why he permits him the sin of fornication. He suggests that it is perhaps God's way of keeping him in his place by proving that he is human and subject to temptation. If that is the case, then he, Holy Willie, will be ready to submit to God's will and endure that imposition. Thus his creed's emphasis on predetermination provides the basis of the logic whereby Holy Willie will continue to 'endure' the pleasures of the flesh while placing all the onus for this with God.

Having apparently confessed and declared himself a penitent, Holy Willie then intercedes with God: 'Lord, bless Thy chosen in this place,/For here Thou has a chosen race'. The repetition of 'chosen' is revealing, implying that Holy Willie feels the need to take comfort from reassurance of his status. Why should he need reassuring? The fury with which he petitions God gives the answer:

> But God confound their stubborn face
>   An' blast their name,
> Wha bring Thy elders to disgrace
>   An' open shame!

Holy Willie's recurrent references to his status ('Thy servant'; 'chosen') betoken a mixture of insecurity and resentment: *why* has the God whom he loyally serves allowed the humiliation of himself and his fellow-elders? Holy Willie's rancour towards Gavin Hamilton is fuelled partly by a sense of his having been let down by God, and his response testifies to both his own limitations and those of his creed:

> Lord, mind Gau'n Hamilton's deserts:
> He drinks, an' swears, an' plays at cartes,
> Yet has sae monie takin arts
>   Wi' great and sma',
> Frae God's ain Priest the people's hearts
>   He steals awa.

> And when we chasten'd him therefore,
> Thou kens how he bred sic a splore,
> And set the warld in a roar
>   O' laughin at us:
> Curse Thou his basket and his store,
>   Kail an' potatoes!

Gavin Hamilton's 'sins', as first cited by Holy Willie, are minor ones indeed – drinking, swearing, and playing cards. The real reason for Holy Willie's hostility is that Hamilton, as an articulate exponent of enlightened doctrine, is winning people away from 'Auld Licht' orthodoxy. What is revealed very clearly here is a belief-system under threat from the challenge of enlightenment. With his fellow-elders Holy Willie has been made a laughing-stock, and he resents the fact that his omnipotent and omniscient God has permitted this to happen. But, unknown to him, the terms of his response show exactly why it happened. A narrow and outmoded orthodoxy, confronted by the humane spirit of enlightenment, can respond to the challenge with nothing but the most mundane of curses. 'Curse Thou his basket and his store/ Kail and potatoes' conveys both Holy Willie's grubby materialism and the severely constrained nature of his theology. It is also fittingly specific in that Hamilton had been summoned before the kirk-session for having his servants gather potatoes on the Sabbath. This absurdly parochial note is maintained in stanza 13 where the Almighty is enjoined to smack the heads of the Presbytery of Ayr for their misdeeds.

With justification, Thomas Crawford has suggested that 'the comedy resides in a clash between the sublime pretensions of the elect and their miserable snivelling when successfully challenged by an assembly of Moderates' (Crawford, *Burns*, p.56). Holy Willie tries to convince himself that Hamilton's triumph has been effected by the rhetoric of his lawyer, 'that glib-tongu'd Aiken', but the truth of the matter he then unwittingly discloses: no mere triumph of rhetoric would cause his heart and flesh to quake at the recollection of the experience. The irony here is particularly telling: the man who is the pillar of the Auld Licht temple and who is confident enough to employ vulgar colloquialisms in his conversation with the Almighty is here revealed by his own testimony as the physical embodiment of terror when confronted by the challenge of a humane creed. Holy Willie's blinkered arrogance is undermined from within. It is precisely because he 'stood sweatin, shakin/An' pish'd wi' dread' that he has to summon up all the virulence of the language of the evangelicals to invoke

God to wreak vengeance on their common enemies, Hamilton and
Aitken:

> Lord, in Thy day o' vengeance try him!
> Lord, visit him wha did employ him!
> And pass not in Thy mercy by them,
>   Nor hear their pray'r,
> But for Thy people's sake destroy them,
>   An' dinna spare!

The thunderous vehemence of this plea for vengeance is
appropriate from one whose theology conceives of a vengeful God.
Here the unremitting force of the language elevates Holy Willie's
status momentarily from the petty to the monstrous. Holy Willie
seems to exist on a par with the tyrannical God whose representative he believes himself to be.

With the final stanza comes another change in tone,
appropriately since Holy Willie's concerns change. Here he
engages in a commercial transaction with the Almighty:

> But, Lord, remember me and mine
> Wi' mercies temporal and divine,
> That I for grace an' gear may shine
>   Excell'd by nane;
> And a' the glory shall be Thine –
>   Amen, Amen!

If, just previously, Holy Willie in his rage was almost the equal of
his vengeful God, then here he appears as the confident, calculating businessman. Self-righteousness and self-interest are fused
inextricably together. Holy Willie's language once again reveals
his priorities. In the controlled movement of the final part of the
prayer the twinning and balancing of terms is especially effective,
reflecting the entrepreneur's care in shaping the deal, his
confidence in its successful outcome, and perhaps also by
implication, his belief in the balanced nature of the relationships
('me and mine'; 'temporal and divine'; 'grace and gear'). As the
concluding 'Amen, Amen!' indicates, Holy Willie has no doubt that
the Almighty will be bought off, successfully bribed by the
promise of 'a' the glory'. If the Almighty rewards Holy Willie then
in return he will be rewarded with his praise.

Thus the conclusion of the poem is superficially a tribute to
God and actually a celebration by Holy Willie of his success. Self-
interest has masqueraded as piety, and the ultimate irony is that
it should have done so using the form and the terminology of

prayer. With no need of explicit comment from Burns, Holy Willie's creed is revealed as a travesty of religion, whose aims, 'grace and gear' (the alliteration implying both their equal status and their inextricable inter-involvement) suggest the readiness of Calvinism to exploit the work-ethic for its own ends.

Without his being aware of it, Holy Willie stands condemned from his own mouth. There has been no need for Burns to intervene to pass judgement (this being a feature of Holy Willie's creed especially inimical to Burns). Both the individual and the doctrine to which he gives voice have been revealed for what they are. Noting the general significance of the specific, David Daiches has commented, 'The point of the poem is not simply that Holy Willie is a hypocrite; it is that some kind of unconscious hypocrisy is made inevitable by the views he professes' (Daiches, *Robert Burns*, p.189). Burns is detached throughout, but this does not mean that he has no views on the subject. We hear Holy Willie's prayer, but by distancing himself and allowing his satiric victim to reveal himself Burns indicates very clearly where he stands on the issue.

There is a respect in which the poet's absence from his poem contributes, paradoxically, to the stature of the speaker. Holy Willie has centre-stage throughout, and he holds forth, uninterrupted, in his address to the Almighty. Almost inevitably, this affords him a certain stature. Indeed there is an essential ambivalence about Holy Willie. From his own words he is shown to be self-righteous, bigoted, and hypocritical; but he has some of the characteristics of the over-reacher, the man who would set himself up alongside the gods. Here, after all, is an individual who, believing himself to be 'a pillar...a guide, a buckler, and example', has the nerve – altogether breath-taking – to enter confidently into negotiations with the Almighty. As the embodiment of monstrous egotism and calculating self-interest, he leaves us with the impression that, notwithstanding his defeat at the hands of enlightened reason, he yet remains a force with which to be reckoned. And we are left with this impression largely because Burns, as master of psychological realism, has presented Holy Willie as an entirely credible human being whose emotions, reactions, and conduct ring true. If the recognisably human can so combine the monstrous and the petty then Burns's point is effectively made.

Burns's versatility in the creation of personae was to serve him well. His range of voices and personae fulfilled a range of functions. Sometimes the speaker is the target of satire,

sometimes its vehicle. In 'The Brigs of Ayr', a poem written in
heroic couplets, the 'Sprites' or spirits of the Auld Brig and the
New Brig (begun May 1786, a few months before the poem's
composition) are personified and meet in dialogue. For this type of
dialogue between personified objects there were precedents in
Scottish poetry, most recently and notably in Fergusson's 'Mutual
Complaint of Plainstanes and Causey' (a debate between a street
and a pavement), 'A Drink Eclogue' (a dialogue between a bottle of
brandy and a bottle of whisky), and 'The Ghaists'. The format
derives from the flyting tradition in which the dialogists try to
outdo one another in their claims for their own achievements and
their demeaning of those of their opponents. As Burns's
personified bridges flyte each other the poem develops into a
vernacular Scots treatment of the generation gap or the ancients-
v.-moderns debate. Representing respectively tradition and
progress, the bridges offer their contrasting views on such subjects as architecture, town-councillors, magistrates, and general
standards of public behaviour. Here the satire is gentler than in
'Holy Willie's Prayer', and Burns effectively balances the view-
points, enabling the reader to sympathise with aspects of each.

Earlier that year (1786) Burns had written 'The Twa Dogs', a
poem in octosyllabic couplets. Initially this poem seems firmly
rooted in the Scottish tradition of animal poetry, a tradition
exemplified in Robert Henryson's *Fables*. Soon, however, it is
revealed as very much a poem of its age – a vigorous social satire
written in an era of revolution. Using vernacular Scots at its most
expressive, Burns first establishes his dogs as dogs: Caesar, a
retriever, is the aristocrat's gun-dog, while Luath is the
ploughman's collie. Unlike their masters, however, the dogs are
not subject to class-barriers:

> Nae doubt but they were fain o' ither,
> And unco pack an' thick thegither;
> Wi' social nose whyles snuff'd an' snowkit;
> Whyles mice an' moudieworts they howkit;
> Whyles scour'd awa' in lang excursion,
> An' worry'd ither in diversion;
> Till tir'd at last wi' monie a farce,
> They sat them down upon their arse,
> An' there began a lang digression
> About the 'lords o' the creation'.

The use of the vernacular to describe each dog helps to emphasise
their natural fellowship and underlines the irony of their

discussing the class-divisions which obtain in the world of their masters. Caesar pities the life of the peasant dog and contrasts life on the laird's estate where even the lowliest servant knows where his next meal is coming from. In response, Luath acknowledges that their life is hard but claims that it has its compensations:

> But how it comes, I never kend yet,
> They're maistly wonderfu' contented;
> An' buirdly chiels, an' clever hizzies,
> Are bred in sic a way as this is.

This may not have been the answer Caesar was expecting, because he then adds insult to injury, presumably in an attempt to provoke Luath into the reaction he wants:

> But then to see how ye're negleckit,
> How huff'd, an cuff'd, an' disrespeckit!
> Lord man, our gentry care as little
> For delvers, ditchers, an' sic cattle;
> They gang as saucy by poor folk,
> As I wad by a stinking brock.

Luath responds with a spirited defence of the life-style of the peasantry in which he claims that, accustomed to poverty, they value their pleasures the greater. He acknowledges, though, that some families are being evicted to enable their masters, courtesy of their more impressive estates, to further their political careers. This prompts Caesar to a vehement indictment of the vanity and corruption inherent in high society.

Caesar's speech marks the turning-point in the dialogue. Thus far, Caesar has seemed to be in control, directing the course of the debate. From this point, however, it is Luath who is in charge. There is real irony in his comment,

> But will ye tell me, master Caesar:
> Sure great folk's life's a life o' pleasure?
> Nae cauld nor hunger e'er can steer them,
> The vera thought o't need na fear them.

The ploughman's collie is now the master of the proceedings. In a splendidly ironic reversal it is Caesar who now defends the natural life-style of the peasantry, contrasting it with the neurosis, boredom, pretension, and debauchery which characterise the life of the gentry. Finally sealing Burns's social critique, the dogs rejoice that 'they were na *men*, but *dogs*' and go their

separate ways. However, true to their natural fellowship, they
resolve 'to meet some ither day'.

Burns's use of dogs to focus on the issue of class-division is a
master-stroke. It is an effective means of identifying the problem,
but of course, as dogs, they are not required to try to solve it; they
can, however, by their behaviour, exemplify an alternative society
where fellowship is the norm. At a time of social unrest Burns is
thus able to highlight social division, but the poem's rhetoric enables
him to embody, rather than directly express, his own attitude. It is
significant, too, that it is Luath, the peasant dog, who gains the
upper hand in the management of the argument. This leads to the
speculation that his responses to Caesar's comment have, from the
outset, been dictated by this end, i.e. he has been quite deliberately
playing Caesar along. On one level the poem may well be a study of
the psychology of power. That it is the farm-dog, Luath, that
emerges as the master of rhetoric may be Burns's subtly oblique
indication of where his hopes for the future lie.

One other example of Burns's use of persona warrants
particular attention as it is by far the most overtly political. In
'Address of Beelzebub' the speaker is the Devil himself. The poem
was prompted by the refusal of a number of Highland landlords to
allow their tenants to emigrate to North America, which would
have meant losing their services on their estates. The epigraph to
the poem gives some sense of the outrage which Burns felt. In the
poem his strength of feeling finds expression in the especially
telling irony of having Beelzebub praise those responsible for
preventing the emigration of the Highlanders, only to raise the
possibility that they may enlist in the cause of freedom in North
America in terms which reveal his, the Devil's, admiration:

> Faith! you and Applecross were right
> To keep the Highland hounds in sight!
> I doubt na! they wad bid nae better
> Than let them ance out owre the water!
> Then up amang thae lakes and seas,
> They'll mak what rules and laws they please:
> Some daring Hancock, or a Franklin,
> May set their Highland bluid a-ranklin;
> Some Washington again may head them,
> Or some Montgomerie, fearless, lead them;
> Till (God knows what may be effected
> When by such heads and hearts directed)
> Poor dunghill sons of dirt an' mire
> May to Patrician rights aspire!

In the virulent irony of the Devil's rebuking Glengary for his leniency, only to proceed to represent in all its enormity the oppression of the poor, there is an intensity of satiric commitment that is redolent of Jonathan Swift:

> But hear, my lord! Glengary, hear!
> Your hand's owre light on them, I fear:
> Your factors, grieves, trustees, and bailies,
> I cannot say but they do gaylies:
> They lay aside a' tender mercies,
> An' tirl the hullions to the birses.
> Yet while they're only poind and herriet,
> They'll keep their stubborn Highland spirit.
> But smash them! crush them a' to spails,
> An' rot the dyvors i' the jails!
> The young dogs, swinge them to the labour:
> Let wark an' hunger mak them sober!
> The hizzies, if they're aughtlins fawsont,
> Let them in Drury Lane be lesson'd!
> An' if the wives an' dirty brats
> Come thiggin at your doors an' yetts,
> Flaffin wi' duds an' grey wi' beas',
> Frightin awa your deuks an' geese,
> Get out a horsewhip or a jowler,
> The langest thong, the fiercest growler,
> An' gar the tatter'd gypsies pack
> Wi' a' their bastards on their back!

After anticipating what 'my Lord' may be capable of, the Devil declares that he is eager to meet him and assures him of his reserved place of honour in hell.

Here Burns has created a persona for expressly political purposes. Noting that this poem was written under the shadow of the American Revolution, Thomas Crawford has suggested that it 'looks forward to the mood of the early seventeen-nineties' and 'is as near to the French spirit as anything else produced by Burns at this period' (Crawford, *Burns*, p.164).

BURNS AND THE SUPERNATURAL

Almost five years separate Burns's two long narrative poems, 'Death and Doctor Hornbook' and 'Tam o' Shanter'. If the latter is Burns's masterpiece the former is of interest both in pointing the way to it and in its own right. Each poem recounts an individual's encounter with the supernatural; each depends for its effect on the creation of a distinct narrative voice; and in each Burns brings his imagination to bear on specific or local circumstances.

The circumstances of the composition of 'Death and Doctor Hornbook', early in 1785, are noteworthy. John Wilson, who taught school in Tarbolton, was the inspiration for Dr. Hornbook. To augment his academic pittance, Wilson had set up a grocer's shop where he also offered his services as an apothecary. Gilbert Burns gave this view of Wilson to James Currie, Burns's editor:

> Having accidentally fallen in with some medical books, and become almost hobby-horsically attached to the study of medicine, he had added the sale of a few medicines to his little trade. He had got a shop-bill printed, at the bottom of which, overlooking his own incapacity, he had advertised that 'Advice would be given in common disorders at the shop gratis' (Kinsley, *Poems and Songs*, III, 1053).

Normally the free 'advice' would lead to the prescription of remedies on sale in his store. Burns seems to have been highly entertained by Wilson's setting himself up as a medical practitioner. In general, Burns was amused by the jargon of the learned professions and the certainty of authorities, and if, as with Wilson, it was authority based on questionable substance, then it became a ready target for satiric attack. After a masonic gathering at which Wilson offered medical judgements with conviction, Burns conceived of the satire.

The title, 'Death and Doctor Hornbook' is apt because it implies a relationship, or even a contest, between the two. A hornbook was an elementary primer listing rudiments such as the alphabet, basic numbers, and the Lord's Prayer. By so naming the amateur apothecary, Burns is indicating that his knowledge is of a most basic kind. The sub-title 'A True Story', sets the context in terms which, as the early stanzas reveal, are decidedly ironic. 'Some books are lies frae end to end', says the narrator, and he notes that 'ev'n ministers', justifying their conduct in terms of 'holy rapture', have been known to sell a great lie by endorsing it with scriptural authority. In contrast, his tale is true, 'just as true's the Deil's in hell/Or Dublin city'. With hindsight, this can be seen to be highly ironic: if Death is on the loose in Ayrshire, how can anyone be certain where the Devil is?

The narrator is rapidly characterised by the way he tells his tale. Though he is adamant he wasn't drunk, the rhythms and syntax of stanza 3 suggest otherwise by mimicking his movements:

> The clachan yill had made me canty,
> I was na fou, but just had plenty;
> I stacher'd whyles, but yet took tent ay
>   To free the ditches;
> An' hillocks, stanes, an' bushes, kend ay
>   Frae ghaists an' witches.

In the fourth stanza he undermines his claims still further by recounting that he could not tell whether the rising moon had three or four horns; and in the fifth he admits that he had difficulty maintaining a straight course. With his brain befuddled by alcohol he encounters 'Something' which induces a fear of ghosts ('pat me in an eerie swither'). But, as Thomas Crawford has observed in a memorable phrase, 'Inebriation is the ideal preliminary for an encounter with the unseen' (Crawford, Burns, p.119).

Death is a strange, awesome figure, with a scythe over one shoulder and a three-pronged fish-spear over the other. Unnaturally tall but of skeletal frame, Death typifies a Scottish tradition of the grotesque which can be traced in literature from the Makars via Ramsay and Fergusson and the caricatures of Smollett to Burns. But what is so striking is that the narrator subjects Death to a process of familiarisation, coming to terms with the unknown by means of the known:

> Its stature seem'd lang Scotch ells twa;
> The queerest shape that e'er I saw,
> For fient a wame it had ava;
>   And then its shanks,
> They were as thin, as sharp an' sma'
>   As cheeks o' branks.

Instead of taking to his heels, the narrator, Burns's common man at his most sociable, greets this grotesque figure courteously and, again relating to the terms of his own experience, remarks on his unseasonal mowing. When Death fails to reply the narrator, ever convivial, invites him to go for a drink. Death then identifies himself but, immediately and unexpectedly, insists that there is no need to be afraid. The narrator, reaching for his knife to defend himself, is assured by Death that he means him no harm, though, as if clinging to the remnants of his pride, he warns that if it did come to a fight he would prove to be a handful.

It is a bizarre situation, a complete reversal of convention. Death, down on his luck, needs a sympathetic listener. Naturally sociable and fortified by alcohol, the narrator fits the bill perfectly. His 'bargain' with Death is to agree to join him for a chat. The traditionally fearsome figure of Death is humanised: like ordinary mortals he needs sympathy; like anyone else he has to work for a living. In a neat irony Burns indicates that Death is of the Auld Licht faction in that he accepts Ussher's dating of the Fall: 'Sax thousand years are near-hand fled/Sin I was to the butching bred'. Death speaks just like a member of the community, using the idioms, rhythms, and oaths of colloquial speech ('And faith! he'll waur me'; 'Ye ken Jock Hornbook i' the clachan?/Deil mak his king's-hood in a spleuchan'). One of Burns's most remarkable achievements in this poem is to accommodate ordinary colloquial speech within poetic form without there being any apparent strain. Perhaps the rhythms of the Standard Habbie stanza-form are especially conducive to this, but it is a significant achievement nonetheless.

Essentially the effect is to localise Death. A levelling process is in operation. Death seems ordinary, almost pathetically so, and the irony of his situation is intensified by the fact that it is from his own lips that we learn of his humiliation. It is Death himself who tells us, 'The weans haud out their fingers laughin,/And pouk my hips', and it is he who relates that he drew his scythe in such a fury at Hornbook that he almost fell over. In contrast, Hornbook's status is elevated to that of a monstrous figure in respect of both his professional arrogance and his actual incompetence. As is indicated in stanza 19, his methods of diagnosis are rather basic. Death reports Hornbook's acquisition of the trappings and terminology of the medical profession, but Burns undermines such pretensions to learning by means of the comic effect of the rhymes in stanza 20 ('whittles', 'mettles', 'bottles', 'rattles') and the combining of Latin terms and the most mundane items in a catalogue of increasingly detailed and increasingly absurd remedies:

'Calces o' fossils, earth, and trees;
True *sal-marinum* o' the seas;
The *farina* of beans an' pease,
      He has't in plenty;
Aqua-fontis, what you please,
      He can content ye.

Forbye some new, uncommon weapons,
Urinus spiritus of capons;
Or mite-horn shavings, filings, scrapings,
      Distill'd *per se*:
Sal-alkali o' midge-tail-clippings,
      And monie mae.'

However the point is lost on the narrator, who predicts that such 'expertise' augurs a bleak future for the local grave-digger. Groaning 'an eldritch laugh', Death sets the record straight: it is he who risks redundancy since Hornbook, thanks to his incompetence in diagnosis and prescription, kills at twenty times the rate Death does. The supernatural power has been reduced to the mundanely human by the monstrous incompetence of one mortal. Thanks to Hornbook the traditionally awesome figure of Death seems in danger of becoming one of the local down-and-outs.

Burns does not leave things there, however. To support his case, Death cites some examples of those dispatched by Hornbook. These also serve Burns's broader purpose of introducing some of his favourite satiric targets – human wickedness and hypocrisy. There are those, it seems, who exploit Hornbook's notorious incompetence for their own ends. The example of the laird's son who inherits by paying Hornbook two ewes to prescribe appropriately for his father's stomach-upset leads one to suspect the motives of the 'honest' wabster who has engaged Hornbook to cure his coarse wife's head-ache. Equally there is sympathy for the innocent victims, such as the girl who, explaining her condition as the effect of 'some ill-brewn drink', seeks to terminate her pregnancy but, courtesy of Hornbook, is consigned to 'her lang hame'.

The poem ends with Death, gathering together the vestiges of his pride, confiding his plan to the narrator before vowing, 'I'll nail the self-conceited sot,/As dead's a herrin'. In contrast with the human deviousness just exemplified, Death, true to his 'bargain', takes his leave of the narrator, letting him go unharmed. In respect of the relationships that have been established the end of the poem is highly ironic. Death and the narrator have met as equals. The chance to pour out his troubles has been useful therapy for Death, and he goes on his way with some of his confidence restored and with the prime aim of taking care of the common enemy, his human rival, Hornbook. By reducing Death and inflating the status of Hornbook, Burns has effectively dramatised his point: it is not Death that is to be feared but Hornbook and those who would hire him for their own corrupt ends. Here, as in 'Tam o' Shanter', Burns suggests that the real causes for concern are in the sphere of human conduct not the realm of the supernatural.

'Tam o' Shanter' is probably the best-known account in world literature of man's encounter with the supernatural. It originated in a fortunate set of circumstances. From childhood Burns had known of the local legends surrounding Alloway Kirk, ruined since late in the seventeenth century and allegedly haunted. In 1789 he met the English antiquarian, Captain Francis Grose, who was collecting material for his *Antiquities of Scotland*. Gilbert Burns later reported the encounter as follows:

> Robert requested of Captain Grose,when he should
> come to Ayrshire, that he would make a drawing of
> Alloway-Kirk, as it was the burial-place of his father,
> and where he himself had a sort of claim to lay down
> his bones...and added, by way of encouragement,
> that it was the scene of many a good story of witches
> and apparitions, of which he knew the Captain was
> very fond. The captain agreed to the request,
> provided the poet would furnish a witch-story, to be
> printed along with it.

In the summer of 1790 Burns sent Grose an account of three local witch-stories. The first two, as he describes them (*Letters*, II, 29–31), contain the nucleus of the poem.

Conspicuously absent from the material sent to Grose is the shrewish wife. Inspiration for Kate came from another source. An acquaintance of Burns, Douglas Graham of Shanter Farm, had explained to his wife his late return home from Ayr in terms of his interrupting a dance of witches at Alloway Kirk.

Together with the legends collected for Grose, this instance was to provide the inspiration for 'Tam o' Shanter', the pre-eminent example of the genre which folk-lorists term the Wild Ride. Tales of encounters with the supernatural occur widely in folk-literature,but Burns's treatment is particularly characterised by sophisticated intelligence and stylistic expertise. These claims will be substantiated in terms of the following: the use of the narrator; the orchestration of language-levels; the relationships between realism and fantasy; the use of elements of the mock-heroic; and the creative synthesis of features of folk-literature, the vernacular poetic tradition, the classical epic, and the early English novel. That sub-title, 'A Tale', is misleadingly bland, and deliberately so.

In the opening lines the narrator sets the context, describing first the street scene at the end of market-day and then the festivities in the inn where 'we sit bousing at the nappy,/An' getting fou and unco happy'. By speaking for, and from, the group,the narrator implies that it is quite normal to celebrate without thinking of the price to be paid (both in terms of the hazardous journey home and the reception therein). In the description of the 'sulky,sullen dame,/Gathering her brows like gathering storm' the simile prefigures the storm which Tam has first to brave, while the metaphor of 'Nursing her wrath to keep it warm' suggests that this is an activity as natural and inevitable as nursing a baby. The contrast is strikingly drawn between the convivial group and the solitary figure feeding her fury. In the 'sulky, sullen dame' is perhaps personified the Calvinist concern with the reckoning to which all human conduct is subject. There may also be an evocation of classical epic and in particular the return of the hero, Odysseus,to account to his wife for his absence of many years. Certainly by this stage the narrator has established the general point that pleasure always has a price which must be paid sooner or later.

With this universal truth established, the narrator then turns to the particular exemplar:

> This truth fand honest Tam o' Shanter,
> As he frae Ayr ae night did canter;
> (Auld Ayr, wham ne'er a town surpasses,
> For honest men and bonie lasses.)

Burns's narrator is characterised by his way of telling the tale. As David Daiches has pointed out (Daiches, *Robert Burns*, p. 252), the narrator is a drinking crony of Tam's. But as well as being a reveller he is also very much the bar-room sage, never stuck for an opinion and always ready to place the particular experience in the context of the general. One of the patterns set up in the poem is the alternation between incident and commentary. With a fund of material for the telling and a captive audience, the narrator can choose exactly how he is going to tell his tale. He relishes both the importance of his function and the licence which it extends to him, the latter enabling him, for instance, to pay a boastful compliment – rather in the manner of pub conversation – to his town of Ayr.

It is important to recognise that the narrator's tongue regularly finds its way into his cheek. Thus the concern for Tam with which the third verse-paragraph opens is feigned (if Tam *had* taken Kate's advice there would have been nothing for the narrator to tell). Proof of the narrator's familiarity with Tam is shown by the fact that he is able to reproduce exactly his wife's stream of reproaches. Kate is a lady of many words, most of which hit the mark: 'She tauld thee weel thou was a skellum,/A blethering, blustering, drunken blellum'. Here is the reductive power of vernacular Scots at its most virulent, with the alliterative and assonantal pattern reinforcing the cumulatively abusive effect. We hear exactly the terms of the flyting which Kate has given Tam. For Tam, any excuse is a good excuse for a drink, and lines 21–28, with their repetition and patterned movement, reproduce precisely Kate's tirade. The narrator also reports Kate's prophecy (a detail redolent of the prefiguring of classical epic) and does so in terms which anticipate the ensuing action. For Kate, to be 'catch'd wi' warlocks in the mirk/By Alloway's auld, haunted kirk' would be to pay a price commensurate with the scale of the offence. Here once again the concern of the poem with the disparity between experience (and particularly convivial pleasure) and judgement of experience surfaces. In effect the reader is invited to ask if life-energies and moral or judgemental codes are so different as to be totally incompatible (like Tam and Kate).

With yet another shift in perspective the ironic appropriateness of this point becomes evident. After reproducing Kate's viewpoint the narrator reminds us of his presence and reverts to playing the pub-philosopher, apparently offering a general judgement but actually with tongue once more in cheek:

> Ah! gentle dames, it gars me greet,
> To think how monie counsels sweet,
> How monie lengthen'd, sage advices
> The husband frae the wife despises!

The earlier feigned concern for Tam has been replaced by feigned regret for the generalised 'husband' and 'wife'.

It is extremely useful from Burns's point of view to have a narrator who likes the sound of his own voice. This lengthy preamble has been effective in setting the scene, introducing the principal characters, creating narrative interest (will Kate be proved right?), and – crucially – characterising the narrator. Above all, it has served to ground the tale of the supernatural in what is identifiably the real world. So the tale may begin. But even in the manner in which this is effected the narrator is further characterised: 'But to our tale'. Involving us – it's *our* tale – he is implying that the delay in getting on with the tale is partly our responsibility. Once again he is exploiting his position as master of a captive audience: he will tell his tale in his own time, but if we agree to listen then we are his accomplices and hence are partly responsible for the vagaries in the telling. This is another instance of a process which recurs throughout the poem – the ironising of the reader/listener by the narrator.

The narrator then proceeds to give an affectionately vivid account of Tam's evening of pleasure in the inn:

> Ae market-night,
> Tam had got planted unco right,
> Fast by an ingle, bleezing finely,
> Wi' reaming swats, that drank divinely.

The vernacular is particularly expressive and it is also appropriate since these are the terms which Tam and his friends would use. Souter Johnie is Tam's 'ancient, trusty, drouthy cronie': the sequence of adjectives reflects Tam's priorities, with the most valued quality – 'drouthy' – occupying pride of place beside the noun. Here, too, Burns uses rhythm and syntax to great effect. The regular movement in lines 45–50 ('And ay the ale...was ready chorus') mimics the steady build-up of pleasure, conviviality, and drink, a point humorously expressed in the line 'And ay the ale was growing better'. This suggests that Tam will be oblivious to the storm outside, but the narrator, adept at building tension, reminds the reader of its ominous presence. However this represents only a momentary check to the triumphal progress to the celebration of conviviality which is the climax of the first major section, or movement, of the poem:

> Care, mad to see a man sae happy,
> E'en drown'd himsel amang the nappy.
> As bees flee hame wi' lades o' treasure,
> The minutes wing'd their way wi' pleasure:
> Kings may be blest, but Tam was glorious,
> O'er a' the ills o' life victorious!

Personified Care is drawn to the proceedings but realises that he is powerless in the presence of such pleasure. Abstractions such

as Care belong to another type of poetry altogether, that of the
Augustans, for instance, and that is precisely Burns's point: in the
presence of the warmth and vibrancy of human fellowship
abstractions have no relevance, while at the same time he is
signalling to the reader that his poem is far removed from
Augustan abstraction and is concerned with the real and specific
experiences of the ordinary man. This is exactly the point of that
concluding couplet with its resounding rhyme, 'glorious/victori-
ous'. The last line reproduces Tam's viewpoint; it is he who
believes that, with enough drink, he could conquer all. But the
irony is an affectionate one, and there is enough to suggest that
for the narrator, and, one suspects, for Burns too, the pleasures of
the ordinary man – good company and abundant ale – are
infinitely preferable to the putative 'blessings' of the monarch.

Rightly, David Daiches has drawn attention to 'how effectively
Burns places his pauses and varies his tempo' (Daiches, *Robert
Burns*, p. 252). At this point there is a lengthy pause, prior to a
marked change in language, pace, and tone:

> But pleasure are like poppies spread:
> You seize the flow'r, its bloom is shed;
> Or like the snow falls in the river,
> A moment white – then melts for ever;
> Or like the Borealis race,
> That flit ere you can point their place;
> Or like the rainbow's lovely form
> Evanishing amid the storm.

With a series of four images of transience the narrator reminds us
that everything is in a state of flux, nothing can endure. For
Edwin Muir, these lines substantiated his thesis of the Scottish
dissociation of sensibility – that since the Reformation, and
increasingly since the Union with the pressure of Anglicisation,
Scots expressed their feelings in Scots vernacular and their
thoughts in standard English. Rather, it seems to me that Burns
chose to have his narrator use English here to offset the triumph
of conviviality and the warmth of human relationships (with
which the narrator has identified) with the cold, formal
inevitability of the undeniable fact of human mortality. Having
shared with his reader in the celebration of the victory of life-
energies over judgemental codes and generalities, he now has to
dwell on the obverse to force both himself and his readers to
accept its stark truth. Hence from the general truth of the
proverbial 'Nae man can tether time or tide', he moves to the

specific example of Tam:

> The hour approaches Tam maun ride:
> That hour, o' night's black arch the key-stane,
> That dreary hour Tam mounts his beast in;
> And sic a night he taks the road in,
> As ne'er poor sinner was abroad in.

The repetition of 'hour' tolls out the fact that Tam, like all of us, is time-bound. Life's journey is made up of a series of particular journeys, and at the end of each there is a reckoning and a price to pay, whether to Kate or at judgement-day. Thus the reference here to the 'poor sinner' is particularly apt. In the tumult of lines 73–76 ('The wind blew...the thunder bellow'd') there is a resounding representation of the might of nature in terms which place Tam's drink-induced 'glory' in a quite different perspective. Here Burns's skill in the management of rhythm and sound is at its most effective: nature at its wildest is rendered through the onomatopoeia of 'rattling showers...darkness swallow'd...thunder bellow'd'. This is an appropriate build-up to the first mention of the Devil himself: on such a night even an innocent child 'might understand,/The Deil had business on his hand' – this clearly contributes to creation of further tension.

Once again there is a shift of focus. Burns orchestrates such changes in perspective expertly. From a sensuous evocation of nature at its most threatening we zoom in on Tam, the ordinary man, whose very ordinariness as it is reflected in language, rhyme, and rhythm has an affectionately comic dimension: 'Weel mounted on his grey meare Meg,/A better never lifted leg'. Yet at the same time there is a heroic dimension to Tam's perseverance: 'Tam skelpit on thro' dub and mire,/Despising wind, and rain, and fire'. The balance between the heroic and the comic, in both Tam and the narrator's attitude to him, is particularly evident here:

> Whiles holding fast his guid blue bonnet,
> Whiles crooning o'er some auld Scots sonnet,
> Whiles glow'ring round wi' prudent cares,
> Lest bogles catch him unawares.

Since Tam, the ordinary man, is our representative he can never be presented in terms that are exclusively heroic; rather, he must be shown to be human and fallible and to react in a normal human way.

Tam is perhaps not just the ordinary man but the ordinary Scot. Thomas Crawford has suggested that 'Tam o' Shanter' 'is –

next to 'The Vision' – the most genuinely *national* of all Burns's
poems' (Crawford, *Burns*, p.222). It might be argued that in lines
83–86 ('Whiles holding...catch him unawares') Tam is the average
Scot presented in the context of some of the defining terms of his
existence – immediate physical circumstances (l.83); artistic
expression (1.84); and the supernatural (ll.85–6). Though Tam is
sufficiently buoyed up by alcohol to scorn the elements, he is still
mindful of the threat which the haunted kirk poses. Pride of place
in that sequence ('Whiles holding...whiles crooning...whiles
glow'ring') is reserved for the supernatural and the fear which it
prompts. The values of Tam and the society to which he belongs
are dominated by superstition and fear of the supernatural;
together these induce a characteristically Presbyterian emphasis
on prudence, circumspection, and humility. Here it is worth
remembering that Burns was writing in 1790, by which point the
ideas of Scottish Enlightenment philosophers had been fairly
widely disseminated. This would suggest that Burns is to some
degree distanced from his creation.

    Various features of the poem foster the reader's credulity,
encouraging acceptance of the transition from the real to the
supernatural. Foremost are the momentum of the narrative,
which derives largely from the verve of Burns's octosyllabic
couplets, and the skilful variation in pace; the depiction of Tam as
the average man (the phrase is Thomas Crawford's) and the use of
his vernacular speech to authenticate his experiences; and the
narrator's mastery of localisation and his eye for particular detail.
Tam's journey is presented in vividly visual terms:

> By this time he was cross the ford,
> Whare in the snaw the chapman smoor'd;
> And past the birks and meikle stane,
> Whare drunken Charlie brak's neck-bane;
> And thro' the whins, and by the cairn,
> Whare hunters fand the murder'd bairn;
> And near the thorn, aboon the well,
> Whare Mungo's mither hang'd hersel.

By the patterned movement of the verse here, Burns ensures that,
step by step, stage by stage, we share Tam's journey; and the
momentum established implies the revelation of ever-worse
enormities. But we look at these landmarks under the guidance of
the narrator so that, sharing his familiarity, we become a member
of the community, a local. The degree of familiarisation introduces
a comic element into this catalogue of horrors. 'Whare drunken

Charlie brak's neck-bane' is funny, and intentionally so. 'Whare hunters fand the murder'd bairn' most definitely is not. But the alliteration in 'Mungo's mither' reintroduces a humorous note. Rapid transitions of mood and emotional fluctuation of this kind are a feature of the Scottish tradition of the grotesque and are to be found in writers as diverse as William Dunbar, Robert Henryson, Tobias Smollett, Robert Fergusson, and Robert Louis Stevenson.

Burns's narrator then gives, in lines 97–100 ('Before him ... thunders roll') a further reminder of the might of the natural world, an appropriate accompaniment to a litany of human evil and tragedy. The effect is to create a level of expectation in the reader: we are invited to anticipate that the catalogue of horrors will reach its climax at Kirk-Alloway. Once again, however, the unexpected is sprung upon us. Though the trees are 'groaning' under the impact of the worst that nature can inflict on them, Kirk-Alloway radiates a light which challenges nature's 'lightnings'. From the allegedly haunted church resound 'mirth and dancing', a phrase which evokes the warmth and sociability which Tam has had to abandon earlier.

Burns's writing is vividly visual. He is here identified as part of a tradition in Scottish literature, that of the dynamic rendering of the pictorial, wherein the writer utilises all his resources of language to depict sights, sounds, and sensations. Typified in the poetry of Dunbar, this quality was revived in poems of Fergusson such as 'Auld Reikie' and 'Leith Races' and in the depiction of crowds in the novels of Smollett. With the verve of the language propelling the reader from scene to scene, the effect is like that of watching a rapid series of vividly detailed slides. But every so often in Burns's poem the narrator reminds us that he is working the projector: he interposes his own thoughts on what he has just presented. Thus that typically Scottish alternation between flux and fixity, motion and stasis, is reflected in the patterned structure of the poem, which alternates between description and commentary. So convincingly is this accomplished that we forget that Burns is pulling the strings which work the narrator. This is truly the art which conceals itself by creating the appearance of artlessness.

Though we long to see the next slide, the narrator halts his narrative and keeps us in suspense. Reverting to his bar-crony role, he offers a mock-formal apostrophe to whisky. There is a comic element in the carefully calculated scale of cost and effect: 'Wi' tippeny, we fear nae evil;/Wi' usquabae, we'll face the Devil!'.

As the ordinary man in the pub, the narrator has worked out
exactly what effect from each drink he can expect for his money.
Ironically, whisky and the Devil are established as equals in
terms of stature. Here the narrator's language is again the
expressive vernacular of pub banter: 'The swats sae ream'd in
Tammie's noddle,/Fair play, he car'd na deils a boddle'. There is
another fine comic detail in the recognition that Maggie, unlike
her master unfortified by drink, needs sharp encouragement to go
on, thus endorsing the traditional belief that animals are more
alert than humans to the presence of the supernatural.

Having exclaimed that 'Tam saw an unco sight!', the narrator
again pauses, enabling the reader to reflect and perhaps consider
the veracity of the 'sight': is it all an alcohol-induced hallucin-
ation? Having appeared to give the reader the freedom to pose
this question, the narrator then effectively decides the issue with
a detailed account of the second of that evening's celebrations,
that of the Devil and his witches. The way in which they are
presented suggests analogies with the earlier party: the witches
and the Devil are almost humanised in that they too need to enjoy
themselves after a busy day.

As their choice of dances indicates, these are patriotic Scottish
witches. (This detail typifies the ingenuity of the poets of the
vernacular revival – Ramsay, Fergusson, and Burns – in finding
metaphors to express their nationalism in a Scotland which was
by then part of the Union). If this alerts us to the possibility that
on one level the poem is a symbolic expression of Scottish life and
values, then it is plainly significant that the Devil has set himself
up in the ruined church and is functioning as the source of
creative energy and the centre of cultural activity. The language
and rhythms of the lines describing his playing, like those
depicting the dancing of the witches, exude vitality, a vitality
rendered by means of vernacular speech, thus identifying the
Devil with the community itself. In the presentation of the Devil
is further evidence of the ambivalence noted earlier: he is
fearsome, certainly ('black, grim, and large'), but he is also 'a
tousie tyke' (which makes him a familiar, rather than awesome,
figure). Likewise the witches, with commendable practical sense,
have solved the problem of illumination by placing a light in the
hand of each corpse, thus enabling them to proceed with
celebrating their activities and displaying their trophies in what
is a comic version of the classical epic's catalogue of the spoils of
victory. The lights also enable 'heroic Tam' (aptly named since he
chooses to remain, rather than fleeing to safety) to witness the

proceedings and identify each of the spoils:

> A murderer's banes, in gibbet-airns;
> Two span-lang, wee, unchristen'd bairns;
> A thief new-cutted frae a rape –
> Wi' his last gasp his gab did gape;
> Five tomahawks wi' bluid red-rusted;
> Five scymitars wi' murder crusted;
> A garter which a babe had strangled;
> A knife a father's throat had mangled –
> Whom his ain son o' life bereft –
> The grey-hairs yet stack to the heft;
> Wi' mair of horrible and awefu',
> Which even to name wad be unlawfu'.
> Three Lawyers' tongues, turned inside out,
> Wi' lies seamed like a beggar's clout;
> Three Priests' hearts, rotten, black as muck,
> Lay stinking, vile, in every neuk.

This passage firmly locates Burns within a Scottish tradition wherein the grotesque can prompt, equally and ambivalently, revulsion and amusement (albeit of a rather grim kind). In this tradition, which descends from the Makars, observation of grotesque detail can elicit either a hybrid response or one that fluctuates, sometimes quite startlingly, between horror and laughter. It may testify to the realism of attitude which informs much Scottish writing that there is recognition of the close inter-relationship of what are often regarded – erroneously – as emotional opposites. For the Scottish writer there are points in the emotional cycle where tragedy goes off the scale and becomes comedy, and vice versa. Here 'A garter which a babe had strangled' and 'The grey-hairs yet stack to the heft' are unequiv-ocally horrific, but the globe-trotting of the Scots witches in their quest for victims (witness the 'tomahawks' and 'scymitars') introduces an undeniably humorous element. Yet, as David Daiches points out,the comic note 'does not lessen the suspense' (Daiches, *Robert Burns*, p. 357). The detail of the tomahawks may have been inspired by Burns's reading of Smollett. In *Humphry Clinker* (1771) Smollett had parodied the Gothic horror-story in his account of Lismahago's experiences at the hands of the North American Indians. In July 1788 Burns wrote that he already had *Roderick Random* and *Humphry Clinker* and praised Smollett's 'incomparable humor' (*Letters*, I, 296), while in the summer of 1790 he informed John Moore that he was planning what he termed 'a Comparative view of You, Fielding, Richardson, and

Smollet (*sic*), in your different qualities and merits as Novel-Writers' (*Letters*, II, 37).

There is a further note of acerbic humour in the climax to the catalogue of horrors when the narrator adopts the rhetorical tactic of declining to do what he then proceeds to do. It would be 'unlawfu' to name the ultimate in atrocities, but here they are:

> Three Lawyers' tongues, turned inside out,
> Wi' lies seamed like a beggar's clout;
> Three Priests' hearts, rotten, black as muck,
> Lay stinking, vile, in every neuk.

These lines function as climax to the catalogue of horrors, indicating that if there is anything worse than the enormities previously listed it is professional corruption. Alexander Fraser Tytler commented that these four lines, 'though good in themselves, yet, as they derive all their merit from the satire they contain, are here rather misplaced among the circumstances of pure horror' (Kinsley, *Poems and Songs*, III, 1362), and Burns accordingly omitted them from the 1793 edition. In fact they are crucial to the satire, but it is a satire which the narrator has created by adding them to what was previously the sequence of horrors as witnessed by Tam; thus they represent not Tam's observations but those of the narrator. In view of Burns's antipathy to professional hypocrisy and corruption it seems likely that the narrator speaks here for the poet himself. In fact, this is the only point in the poem when one senses the obtrusive presence of the poet. It is, however, a particularly effective barb, and Burns may well have decided – probably with justification – that its inclusion more than compensated in terms of satire for the momentary loss of narrative authenticity.

The next verse-paragraph (lines 143–150) sees another marked contrast in pace, tone, and perspective. From the horrors we are now directed to, firstly, Tam, the fascinated spectator, and then, at greater length, to the account of the music and dancing. The pace has increased noticeably, and the very rhythm and syntax of the lines mimic the activities which they render:

> As Tammie glowr'd, amaz'd, and curious,
> The mirth and fun grew fast and furious;
> The piper loud and louder blew,
> The dancers quick and quicker flew,
> They reel'd, they set, they cross'd, they cleekit,

– in that last line in particular, the sound pattern and the rhythm enact the sense. Again the witches are humanised: the exertions that have been so vividly represented mean that they too perspire, hence they shed their outer garments.

All along, the narrator has been building up suspense as he depicts the activities which Tam has been witnessing, to the extent that the reader, understandably, wishes to learn of Tam's response. We are denied this, however, as the narrator once again asserts his authority over the narrative. Halting the account, he puts the events in freeze-frame while, resuming his public-bar manner, he boasts to Tam of what he would have done if only the witches had been 'queans,/A' plump and strapping in their teens'. The reality is somewhat different, however, and here again his language is the expressive vernacular of bar-room bluster:

> But wither'd beldams, auld and droll,
> Rigwoodie hags wad spean a foal,
> Louping and flinging on a crummock,
> I wonder did na turn thy stomach!

The joke is on the narrator, however. In flaunting his authority as narrator by stopping the account to indulge in speculation and boasting, he has unwittingly created the conditions for proving his own fallibility. While hypothesising, he has missed out on a vital detail which has certainly not eluded his hero, the enthusiastic spectator Tam, a point which, charitably, the narrator acknowledges: 'But Tam kend what was what fu' brawlie:/There was ae winsome wench and wawlie'.

Having tantalised us with this promising introduction, the narrator once again flexes his muscles and tries our patience by choosing to switch his focus from the ongoing activities to the subsequent career of the young witch. This, of course, is not what we have been geared up to expect, nor is it what we want to hear. However, his reference to her shaking 'baith meikle corn and bear' [barley] reminds us that, traditionally, storms were raised by witches, which prompts the thought that the storm through which Tam earlier battled may have been brewed up by these same witches as accompaniment to their revelry. Restoring the focus of the narrative to the present, the narrator notes both the shortness of the young witch's smock and the pride with which she wears it since it displays her to fullest advantage. Yet again he halts the narrative, this time to address the young witch herself:

Ah! little kend thy reverend grannie,
That sark she coft for her wee Nannie,
Wi' twa pund Scots ('twas a' her riches),
Wad ever grac'd a dance of witches!

This serves two functions: in humorous fashion it emphasises just how short the sark must now be on the full-grown young woman, thus preparing us for the excitement which she stimulates; at the same time it shows that the narrator regards the witch as essentially a human being (for instance, she has a kind granny who has spent all her savings on the gift of the smock). This may simply testify to the intense and natural feeling of sexual attraction which the narrator feels towards her. But Burns may also be suggesting (as with the dancing and sweating earlier) how readily the supernatural may be assimilated into the human (at least in terms of our perception).

Once again the narrator feels the need to pause and so he halts the narrative: 'But here my Muse her wing maun cour,/Sic flights as far beyond her power'. Either this is an admission of his intense excitement or it is an acknowledgement of his limitations as poet. Either way, the point is rhetorical since, courtesy of his Muse, he has already made plain the effect of Nannie on him; hence he proceeds to describe her effect on both Tam and the Devil. This verse paragraph ('But here...the hellish legion sallied') is replete with ironic detail; for instance, 'Tam stood like ane bewitch'd'. Satan himself is subject to the temptations of the flesh: 'Even Satan glowr'd, and fidg'd fu' fain,/And hotch'd and blew wi' might and main'. Here the pace and the rhythm reflect both the increasing tempo of the music and the Devil's mounting sexual excitement. Tam becomes so appreciative of Nannie's dancing that he 'roars out' his approval: '"Weel done, Cutty-sark!"'. The terms used at this point are highly significant with respect to the great eighteenth-century debate, Reason v. Nature: 'Tam tint [lost] his reason a' thegither'. As long as Tam is ruled by his reason he remains undetected, silently relishing the spectacle. As he increasingly and quite naturally succumbs to the lure of the sensual so his instinct gains the upper hand and leads to his cry of excitement.

This marks the climax to the poem but, true to the ambivalence which has recurred throughout, it does so in a way that is strikingly paradoxical. On the one hand, it is highly ironic that Tam's natural, instinctive reaction produces an outburst which leads to his immediate detection, terminates both his enjoyment of the scene and the witches' pleasure in their celebration, and places his life in jeopardy. And just as there is a price to pay for his earlier revelry in having to confront his shrewish wife, so there is the ultimate price to pay for his voyeuristic presence at the witches' revels. But, conversely, Tam with his cry of delight has effectively seized control of the narrative from the narrator. His only words in the poem prompt the instantaneous response which will dictate the subsequent course of the narrative and propel it to its conclusion. For the reader this imposition of direction may come as something of a relief, especially since our narrator has become so enamoured of his licence as narrator as to have become worryingly unreliable (What has happened to his priorities? How could he have missed Cutty Sark? Has he become over-fond of the sound of his own voice?).

It would be tempting to answer that last question in the affirmative on the basis of the verse-paragraph which follows:

> As bees bizz out wi' angry fyke,
> When plundering herds assail their byke:
> As open pussie's mortal foes,
> When, pop! she starts before their nose;
> As eager runs the market-crowd,
> When 'Catch the thief!' resounds aloud:
> So Maggie runs, the witches follow,
> Wi' monie an eldritch skriech and hollo.

This passage is rooted in paradox: to render rapid, furious movement the narrator employs the expanded, or multiple, epic simile: As...as...as...so... . Frantic pursuit is conveyed by means of three analogies. Of these, two (the bees and the market-crowd) evoke earlier moments in the poem, thus introducing a further element of pattern. Together with the multiple exemplification of the central point, this serves to slow the action so that the reader is invited to contemplate ferocious speed in slow-motion.

Ironically, the narrator's next exclamation seems to imply that he has now abdicated his position of authority and is helpless to shape the course of events:

> Ah, Tam! Ah, Tam! thou'll get thy fairin!
> In hell they'll roast thee like a herrin!
> In vain thy Kate awaits thy comin!
> Kate soon will be a woefu' woman!

Now the events described are past history and the narrator, since
he is telling the tale, presumably knows the outcome. How, then,
are we to explain these lines and also his encouragement to Meg –
'do thy speedy utmost' – as if to imply that the result may yet be
determined? Either he has completely lost his grip on the
narrative (and it is at the mercy of a horse!) or else – and much
more likely in view of the humorous hints (in, for instance, the
rhymes 'fairin/herrin' and 'comin/woman') – he is pretending to be
so involved in the vivid present of the action as to share the
limited perspective of its participants. There is a further irony,
though of a different kind in that it relates to the characters
rather than the narrator, in that the very energies which have
sustained Nannie's frenzied dance and stimulated Tam's outburst
also enable her to lead the pursuit which threatens Tam's
survival. Tam's life now depends on a contest between two females
– the witch, Cutty Sark, and Maggie, the mare – and this typifies
the extent to which, throughout, Tam has been subject to female
influences – Kate, Kirkton Jean, Cutty Sark, and Maggie.
Maggie's heroic efforts deliver her master safely, but at the cost of
her tail, a crucial detail because every encounter with the
supernatural has to be corroborated by visible proof.

   With his hero delivered safely from the threat of the
supernatural, the narrator's task is over – but not quite! True to
the conventions of the morality tale and also typical of the spirit of
much Augustan poetry, the narrator chooses to point the moral,
which in this case is a warning against alcohol and womanising:

> Now, wha this tale o' truth shall read,
> Ilk man, and mother's son, take heed:
> Whene'er to drink you are inclin'd,
> Or cutty sarks run in your mind,
> Think! ye may buy the joys o'er dear:
> Remember Tam o' Shanter's meare.

How seriously is this to be taken? – It might be said that the
narrator's neat little homily sounds like a more restrained version
of one of Kate's tirades. As such it is ironic coming from someone
who has identified himself as a drinking-crony of Tam and who
has indicated very clearly the effect which the attractive young
witch had on him. At the conclusion more than anywhere else in
the poem the narrator's tongue is most definitely in his cheek. The
ostensible moral is a sober warning of the kind that might well
find favour with his Presbyterian elders and betters. The actual
import of the poem is a celebration of instincts and energies, both

human and supernatural.

'Tam o 'Shanter' proves that Burns's relationships with his community could produce imaginative literature of the very highest order. In this poem Burns universalises on the basis of a closely contextualised account of the experiences of an ordinary individual. Burns's triumph is in making 'heroic' Tam our representative. In accounting for his success we confront once again the range of influences which Burns first absorbed and then used imaginatively. In the poetry of Ramsay and Fergusson, Burns saw exemplified the process of inflation and reduction, a process that was at the very heart of the Scottish poetic tradition. Both Ramsay and Fergusson had achieved original effects from the tension between classical modes and forms and the distinctly Scottish subject-matter presented by means of them. Just as Burns followed their example in undermining formal English by means of vernacular Scots, so in 'Tam o' Shanter' he achieves, as they had done, a comparably reductive effect by juxtaposing mode and subject-matter. The ordinary man's adventures on the way home from the pub are presented courtesy of the trappings of epic (epic apostrophe; extended simile; epic catalogue).

Such evidence proves Burns's familiarity with classical epic (and there is further corroboration in his correspondence with Mrs. Dunlop, where they discuss the relative merits of Dryden's Virgil and Pope's Homer). These epic translations, providing examples of sustained narrative, were among the ancestors of the English novel. Here we can identify another of the shaping influences on 'Tam o' Shanter' – the comic-epic mode as employed by the early English novelist, Henry Fielding. There are various references to Fielding in Burns's letters, and passages where he mimics Fielding's mock-heroic style.

In 'Tam o' Shanter', then, two traditions meet – that of the vernacular revival in poetry, and the comic-epic as exemplified in the early English novel. The common ground is the clash of manner and matter, which manifests itself in terms of a series of relationships – form v. content; formal language v. colloquial or vernacular speech; and detail v. generalisation, or incident v. commentary. In Book IV, chapter 8 of *Tom Jones* (1748) Fielding describes a fight in the village churchyard in which Molly Seagrim confronts the locals. Fielding follows the elaborate conventions of classical epic in describing the battle, but the actual details are mundane. The effect of this disparity is to elevate the status of the otherwise-ordinary participants, so much so that this has become the definitive account in all literature of the village brawl. Burns's use of the conventions of epic in 'Tam o' Shanter' has a comparably mythopoeic effect: Tam, finally heading home after a few drinks too many, defying the elements, transfixed by the witches' dance until his instincts get the better of him, becomes our representative. By establishing Tam's ordinariness and depicting his responses as recognisably and humorously human, Burns ensures that we can identify with Tam; hence we are likely to believe the account of his experiences. By comically employing some of the features of epic to render those experiences, Burns succeeds in universalising their significance. It is a triumph of the use of technique to shape reader-response.

There is another major respect in which Burns's reading of early English fiction influenced the writing of 'Tam o' Shanter'. It has already been noted that Burns's narrator likes the sound of his own voice and latterly seems to lose his earlier control of his material. In Sterne's *Tristram Shandy* (1759–60) Burns had encountered a narrator who is incorrigibly digressive, often unreliable, and, by conventional standards, far from competent. So convincingly is Tristram presented that if the reader suspects he is being led on a wild goose chase then he is likely to place the onus on Tristram: the incompetence is his, not Sterne's. Similarly, in *Tom Jones* Fielding creates a verbose narrator who, in the belief that he is something of a sage, is forever fussing around the reader, giving directions as to the wider and deeper significance of his material Much of this 'guidance' is proved by events to be unreliable. However Fielding so succeeds in creating an independent narrator that he can effectively disclaim responsibility. Is this not exactly what Burns does in 'Tam o' Shanter'? On one level his 'tale' may be regarded as representing the culmination of the folk-tradition, but there is equal validity in setting it alongside sophisticated experiments in narration such as *Tristram Shandy* and *Tom Jones*, where what is told is important but how it is told is equally so. Indeed the whole poem is rooted in a paradox: the poem's rhetoric (including the comic-epic machinery and the narrator) encourages us to believe, whereas ultimately the poet, distanced by that rhetoric, is saying to us, 'Believe it if you will'.

Perhaps the real 'moral', then, is rooted in the play of possible ways of seeing; in which case, no subject-matter could be more appropriate than the human's journey from the real to the supernatural. The poem offers alternatives: one is that supernatural creatures are more like us than we perhaps realise; the other is that, because of our limitations of understanding, we habitually relate the unknown or supernatural to the known (hence the importance of the landmarks on the journey to Kirk-Alloway and through the poem). Which of these is 'correct'? Part of the fascination of Burns's poem is that it gives rise to this question but it does not impose an answer on the reader.

Earlier it was suggested that Burns's dramatic talent found expression in the creation of a range of poetic voices or personae. The significance of this process was not exclusively literary. In terms of Burns's own psychology it might be said that his dramatic capacity served to render his multiple identity. Thus the more fertile that capacity, the greater the problem of both self-definition and re-integration of the various alternative selves.

A psychological reading of Burns would find much of interest in those poems in which Death or the Devil makes an appearance. In 'Tam o' Shanter' the Devil establishes himself in Kirk-Alloway, the church in which the poet's father was buried and in which the poet himself, as we have noted, 'had a sort of claim to lay down his bones'. As a source of intense creative energy, the Devil has obvious affinities with the poet himself. Could it be that in the figures of Tam, the Devil, and the narrator, Burns is externalising his own internal conflict (in which context the recurrent contrasting of interior and exterior, warmth and storm, has particular relevance)? Could it also be that in the play of relationships among these figures (as also with Death and the narrator in 'Death and Doctor Hornbook') Burns is attempting to establish some measure of equilibrium amongst otherwise-conflicting elements within himself? In identifying poet and Devil as sources of creative energy (and each may be said to represent an alternative creator to the original creator, God) is Burns, by means of that kinship, forging a stable identity, an identity which derives exclusively from his function as poet, or alternative creator? It is revealing that Burns wrote to James Dalrymple, on receiving a rhyming epistle from him, 'I suppose the devil is so elated at his success with you that he is determined by a coup de main to effect his purposes on you all at once in making you a Poet' (*Letters*, I, 93). Here the kinship is openly acknowledged: poets are the Devil's men.

Consideration of 'Address to the Deil' (written winter 1785) is germane to this line of argument. It, too, represents an externalisation of something internal. Taken together, the title and the epigraph give a sense of the contrast which is integral to Burns's method. The vernacular 'Deil' of the title seems at odds with the awesome figure of the epigraph, 'O Prince! O Chief of many throned pow'rs!/That led th' embattled seraphim to war' (Milton,

Paradise Lost, i, 128–9). This reverential attitude is Burns's point of departure and, typically, he is at his most ingenious when he has an orthodox view against which to react. Here he reacts by contrasting, on the one hand, Milton's version of the Fall and recurrent references to scripture and, on the other hand, accounts of the activities of the Devil and witches which derive from folk-lore and popular superstition. These are allowed to interact, and the target of satiric attack is not Milton or the Bible but the austere authority of Calvinism in whose hell-fire sermons the Devil appears as an unremittingly vengeful force.

From the outset Burns's lively use of the vernacular makes of the Devil a merely mischievous figure. Far from being Milton's 'prince', he is 'Auld Hornie', 'Nick', 'Clootie', 'Auld Hangie', 'Auld Nickie-Ben'. The idioms and folk-lore of the rural community are the means of reducing the 'chief of many throned powers'. Here the Devil is not only humanised, he is localised, becoming a member of the community, a crony for whom the speaker plainly has no high regard. From the early stanzas it would seem that in this case familiarity has brought something close to contempt, and the jaunty rhythms of the Standard Habbie stanza are very effective in conveying it. By reducing the Devil to the sum of his achievements, Burns reveals him to be little more than the neighbourhood nuisance.

How could one either fear or revere the figure presented in the opening stanza? The 'devilment' amounts to splashing boiling water about the kitchen (and the rhymes 'Clootie/sootie/cootie' have a comically belittling effect). In stanza 2 the speaker is heavily ironic:

> I'm sure sma' pleasure it can gie,
>   Ev'n to a deil,
> To skelp an' scaud poor dogs like me
>   An' hear us squeel.

Thereafter he presents a catalogue of the Devil's activities, drawing on superstition and demonology for details (roaring like a lion; flying on the wind; haunting ruins; and groaning 'wi' eldritch croon'). Throughout, however, comic details undermine any sinister potential in these activities. For instance the speaker cites his 'rev'rend graunie' and one wonders if she would discuss him so openly if she were truly fearful of the Devil. The terms in which her attitude and his activities are depicted in stanza 6 are scarcely reverential: 'Aft yont the dyke she's heard you bummin,/ Wi' eerie drone'. Likewise, the speaker recounts how he merely 'gat a fright' when 'Ye, like a rash-buss [clump of rushes] stood in sight,/Wi' waving sugh'. The narrator admits to momentary fear, but this is offset immediately by the terms in which he describes the behaviour of the Devil:

> When wi' an eldritch, stoor 'quaick, quaick',
>   Amang the springs,
> Awa ye squatter'd like a drake,
>   On whistling wings.

The arch-demon of hell-fire fame is doing duck impersonations.

Gilbert Burns told James Currie that 'the curious idea of such an address was suggested to [Burns] by running over in his mind the many ludicrous accounts and representations we have, from various quarters, of this august personage'.[7] Thus, of course, he rapidly ceases to be 'august'. In each of stanzas 9–14 Burns gives examples of the activities of the Devil and his cohorts: riding 'on ragweed nags' (even the sound is reductive) and digging up the dead ('howkit dead', rhyming with 'wicked speed' is comically grotesque rather than horrific); draining the milk from cattle; rendering useless the 'wark-lume' of the young husband (here the sexual reference is quite blatant); sending water-kelpies to lure travellers; using 'spunkies' (jack-o'-lanthorns) to lead the drunkard into the mud from which he will never surface; and taking the youngest brother from a family unless mollified by a cockerel or a cat. Paraphrased, some of these actions may sound fearsome, but rendered in vernacular Scots they are familiarised and lose their threat.

The Old Testament account of the Creation, the Temptation, and the Fall provides the inspiration for Milton's great epic poem, *Paradise Lost*. When Burns offers his version it is, typically, a familiar one:

> Lang syne in Eden's bonie yard,
> When youthfu' lovers first were pair'd,
> An' all the soul of love they shar'd,
>   The raptur'd hour,
> Sweet on the fragrant flow'ry swaird,
>   In shady bow'r.

This touching description is immediately contrasted with the demeaning terms and harshly reductive sounds that represent the Devil's part in the Temptation and the Fall (especially the rhymes, 'dog/incog/brogue/shog'). Addressing him as a familiar, the speaker recalls the Devil's treatment of Job ('the man of Uzz') in words whose sense and sound are uniformly demeaning:

> D'ye mind that day when in a bizz
> Wi' reekit duds, an' reestit gizz,
> Ye did present your smoutie phiz
>   'Mang better folk;
> An' sklented on the man of Uzz
>   Your spitefu' joke?

> An' how ye gat him i' your thrall,
> An' brak him out o' house an' hal',
> While scabs an' botches did him gall,
>   Wi' bitter claw;
> An' lows'd his ill-tongu'd wicked scaul –
>   Was warst ava?

This account enables the speaker to show that even Biblical testimony reveals the Devil as a petty and malicious meddler. Having reduced the Devil by means of highly expressive vernacular idiom, the speaker, ironically, claims that it is beyond the competence of 'a Lallan tongue, or Erse,/In prose or rhyme' to render the scope and scale of the Devil's achievements.

In the last two stanzas the speaker takes his leave of the Devil. Here the tone changes subtly. There is an affectionate note in the name, 'Auld Cloots', though it is certainly no more respectful than any of the earlier nicknames. Again the Devil is familiarised and becomes the speaker's crony, to the very extent that the speaker claims he knows what he's thinking (which is that he (the speaker) has had so much to drink that he's havering and will end up in his (the Devil's) black pit); but the speaker vows that he'll 'jink' out of his way and so 'cheat' him. In the final stanza the speaker both bids the Devil adieu and wishes him well. In particular, he expresses the wish that the Devil may, on reflection, mend his ways. Perhaps, he ventures, even the Devil might have a chance to change for the better. He concludes with an expression of compassion: even the Devil does not deserve to have to endure forever the torments of 'yon den', his 'black pit'.

Here is the ultimate challenge to orthodox Calvinist doctrine, which deals in terms of fixed, and often dire, certainties. As if it were not enough to demystify the Devil by showing him to be no more than a pest, Burns has his speaker – once again sounding like his 'ordinary man' – speculate on the possibility of redemption for the Devil. Here is the contemporary doctrine of sympathy taken to its most logical and most practical extreme:

who is in greater need of sympathy and redemption than the Devil, and whose redemption could be of greater benefit to man than the Devil's? On one level it is wittily ingenious – a blatant inversion of the dogma by which Burns was surrounded – but on a serious level it is the most moving exemplification of the generous and compassionate nature of his own brand of religion. Could the Devil, for his sake, somehow be saved? – There is more than a hint here of the redemptive tendency at the heart of Romanticism.

Burns's speaker seems to warm to the Devil because of his weakness and his fallibility. He is not in awe of him, but rather amused by him, and he is able to identify with his human characteristics: if this is the Devil then he is decidedly ordinary, almost touchingly so. William Blake wrote in 'The Marriage of Heaven and Hell',

> The reason Milton wrote in fetters when he wrote of Angels and God, and at liberty when of Devils and Hell, is because he was a true Poet and of the Devil's party without knowing it.

The critic, William Montgomerie, was the first to suggest that Satan had a similar attraction for Burns.[8] The final stanza of 'Address to the Deil' might indicate that the speaker has a vested interest in securing the Devil's salvation.

Collectively, Burns's poems and letters reveal an ambivalent attitude to the Devil, and Burns's fluctuating response was to play a vital part in his own quest for a stable identity among the multiplicity of alternative selves. When Burns felt himself to be an outsider or outcast he readily identified, usually admiringly, with the Devil. For instance, Jean Armour's family's hostility to him drew this response:

> If any thing had been wanting to disgust me compleatly at Armour's family, their mean, servile compliance would have done it. Give me a spirit like my favourite hero, Milton's Satan,

> 'Hail, horrors! hail,
> Infernal world! and thou, profoundest Hell,
> Receive thy new possessor! one who brings
> A mind not to be changed by *place* or *time*!'

Significantly, Burns instantly adds, 'I cannot settle to my mind' (*Letters*, I, 121). Feeling alienated both in Edinburgh and on his return to Ayrshire, he wrote,

> I have bought a pocket Milton which I carry
> perpetually about with me, in order to study the
> sentiments – the dauntless magnanimity; the
> intrepid, unyielding independance; the desperate
> daring, and noble defiance of hardship, in that great
> Personage, Satan (*Letters*, I, 123).

Three years later (8 August 1790) in seeking terms to describe his
condition, he offered a rather different version:

> ...the resemblance that hits my fancy best is, that
> poor, blackguard Miscreant, Satan, who, as Holy
> Writ tells us, roams about like a roaring lion,
> seeking, *searching*, whom he may devour (*Letters*, II,
> 44).

The parallels with the chameleon Burns's quest for his own
identity through the myriad of self-dramatised selves are obvious.
When Burns tried to explain to Mrs. McLehose what he had
meant by saying Satan was 'a favorite hero' of his, he may have
indulged in an element of romanticising:

> My favorite feature in Milton's Satan is, his manly
> fortitude in supporting what cannot be remedied – in
> short, the wild broken fragments of a noble, exalted
> mind in ruins (*Letters*, I, 198).

Nonetheless there is evidence here of his identifying Satan's
mental fragmentation and chameleon nature with his own. For
the critic Lionel Trilling, uncertainty about the self is one of the
characteristics of the modern condition.[9] If Trilling is right, then
Burns's poem and letters, offering as they do a wide range of
voices, would seem to identify Burns as essentially modern.

BURNS AND SONG

Burns wrote many songs and he adapted or reset many more. At his disposal were many traditional airs and numerous sets of lyrics. Two aspects of Burns's achievement in song are particularly noteworthy. One was his ability to write words for existing music – the reverse of normal practice, and considerably more difficult. The other is the range of his songs, from passionate love lyrics to rousing drinking songs and songs of freedom. In the collections to which he contributed, James Johnson's *Scots Musical Museum* and the *Select Collection* of George Thomson, he was aware of the need to maintain a balance. For instance, he wrote to Thomson,

> Your Collection of Sentimental and pathetic songs is, in my opinion, very compleat; but not so your Comic ones. – Where is Tullochgorum, Lumps o' puddins, Tibbie Fowler, Rattlin roarin Willie, and several others, which in my humble opinion, are well worthy of preservation (*Letters*, II, 206).

Familiar with Scots song from infancy, Burns was influenced by the prevalent antiquarian fervour on his first visit to Edinburgh late in 1786. His tours of the Borders and the West Highlands in the summer of 1787 convinced him of the need to preserve native Scots songs and provided him with a wealth of material. This letter of August 1787 to William Tytler reflects both Burns's antiquarian zeal and his determination, at least at this stage, to preserve the material in the form in which he found it:

> Inclosed I have sent you a sample of the old pieces that are still to be found among our Peasantry in the West. I once had a great many of these fragments and some of these here entire; but as I had no idea then that any body cared for them, I have forgot them. – I invariably hold it sacriledge to add any thing of my own to help out with the shatter'd wrecks of these venerable old compositions; but they have many various readings. – If you have not seen these before, I know they will flatter your true old-style Caledonian feelings (*Letters*, I, 147).

By the autumn of 1787 Burns was assisting James Johnson with the further compilation of the *Scots Musical Museum* (the first volume had appeared in May of that year). Soon he was enthusing

to the Reverend John Skinner (whom he addressed as 'the Author
of the best Scotch song ever Scotland saw'),

> There is a certain something in the old Scotch songs,
> a wild happiness of thought and expression, which
> peculiarly marks them, not only from English songs,
> but also from the modern efforts of song-wrights, in
> our native manner and language (*Letters*, I, 167).

In his collaboration with Johnson, Burns was largely
successful in preserving these qualities, but he was less so in his
dealings with George Thomson. In response to Thomson's request
that he help with the *Select Collection* Burns was forthright in
setting out his terms:

> ...if you are for *English* verses, there is, on my part,
> an end of the matter. – Whether in the simplicity of
> *the Ballad*, or the pathos of *the Song*, I can only hope
> to please myself in being allowed at least a
> sprinkling of our native tongue (*Letters*, II, 149).

However he conceded that English verses of merit by Scottish
composers would be admissible. By January 1793 he had given
some ground and he had to argue more vigorously (and,
paradoxically, in formal English) for the preservation of the
distinctive Scots features:

> If it were possible to procure songs of merit, I think
> it would be proper to have one set of Scots words to
> every air, – and that the set of words to which the
> notes ought to be pricked. – There is a naiveté, a
> pastoral simplicity, in the slight intermixture of
> Scots words and phraseology, which is more in
> unison (at least to my taste, and I will add, to every
> genuine Caledonian taste,) with the simple pathos,
> or rustic sprightliness, of our native music, than any
> English verses whatever (*Letters*, II, 181).

Three months later he was enjoining Thomson,

> ...let our National Music preserve its native
> features. – They are, I own, frequently wild, and
> unreduceable to the more modern rules; but on that
> very eccentricity, perhaps, depends a great part of
> their effect (*Letters*, II, 211).

As with poetry, so too with song, Burns was trying to reconcile two traditions, that of the native folk-song and that of polite taste. Despite his earlier strictures he did make concessions to Thomson's demand for refinement and anglicisation. Some of his letters reveal him as a self-conscious artist rather than a natural and unaffected songsmith. Here he promotes simplicity, but from the vantage-point of deliberate and distanced artistry:

> Your other objections to this song will vanish, when you consider that I have not painted Miss Mc—— in the rank which she holds in life, but in the dress and character of a Cottager; consequently the utmost simplicity of thought and artistry was necessary (*Letters*, II, 228).

Of 'Geordie's Byre' he commented, 'The sprinkling of Scotch in it, while it is but a sprinkling, gives it an air of rustic naiveté, which time will rather increase, than diminish' (*Letters*, II, 246). Though such comments on his methods may cause concern to purists, the majority of the songs themselves testify to Burns's success in achieving a perfect consonance of words and music.

Burns is renowned for writing some of the most expressive love lyrics in existence. Probably the best known is 'A Red, Red Rose'. It is a triumph of assimilation. Noting that there were chapbook models for every stanza, James Kinsley rightly claims that it is 'an exquisite example of Burns's art in raising folksong to perfection' (Kinsley, *Poems and Songs*, III, 1454). It is unsurpassed as a simple, moving, and intense statement of undying love. The repetition in the first line is inspired – 'O, my luve's like a red, red rose'. The simile itself is a commonplace but Burns transforms it by the repetition of 'red', so intensifying the effect and requiring the reader to look again at a rose and savour the depth of feeling which the image renders. The song derives its effect from comparisons of telling simplicity, for instance the rose and the sweetly played melody. Burns was familiar with the work of James Hutton in initiating the study of geology and this may well have inspired the imagery of stanza 3 where the elemental terms movingly convey the original and eternal nature of the love:

> Till a' the seas gang dry, my Dear,
> And the rocks melt wi' the sun!
> O I will luve thee still, my Dear,
> While the sands o' life shall run.

The line of connotation – 'seas…rocks…sands o' life', with the last of these evoking the sands of time in the hourglass – is brilliantly managed, conveying the notion that his love stands comparison with original elements but is doubly intense because he is mortal and time-bound. This is mortal man's statement of eternal love. In the final stanza he takes leave of his beloved, but he reaffirms the undying nature of his love, this time in terms of distance as well as duration. Rightly, David Daiches detects in this poem 'that combination of swagger and tender protectiveness so characteristic of the male in love' (Daiches, *Robert Burns*, p.312). The point is that this is real, not idealised, love. It is because it is recognisably an individual's response – deep and genuine – that it has such universal significance.

The authentic voice of intense individual feeling also informs 'Ae Fond Kiss'. The occasion of the song was the departure late in 1791 to rejoin her husband in the West Indies of Mrs. Agnes (Nancy) McLehose, with whom Burns had enjoyed an intensely emotional relationship. To a poignant Gaelic air entitled 'Rory Dall's Port', Burns wrote the words which expressed his feelings at the inevitably sad parting. In the opening lines the repetition of 'ae' and the rhyming of 'sever' and 'forever' reinforce the sense of anguished leave-taking, and the image of the war between 'sighs' and 'groans' conveys the emotional turmoil of the speaker. This song highlights, and particularly in stanza 2, the difference between song as printed text and song in performance. The syntactical inversions in stanza 2 read awkwardly on the page, but the problem vanishes in performance, such is the harmony between musical sound and verbal sense. Of the music, John Ashmead and John Davison have noted, 'The many upward and downward leaps create a kind of keening or sobbing effect, and their large intervals express the sorrow of this final farewell'.[10] In stanza 3 syntax and repetition combine to convey intensity of feeling – 'But to see her was to love her,/Love but her, and love for ever' – with the emphasis on the declining fall of the last three, crucial, terms. Likewise, stanza 4 – for Scott 'the essence of a thousand love tales' (Low, *Burns: Critical Heritage*, p. 208) – reflects both a consummate union of words and music and a subtly effective patterning within the language itself: the repetition of lines 1 and 2 focuses attention on the only two words that differ, 'kindly' and 'blindly', and the haunting repetition of 'never' heightens the sense of mental anguish. The mood changes in stanza 5 as the speaker wishes his beloved all happiness in the future. Here again, patterned repetition directs attention to the words which are not repeated, 'first and fairest' and 'best and dearest'. The final stanza seems to replicate the first, but with one subtle change: 'alas' replaces 'and then' in line 2. The effect is to convey his awareness that the final parting, delayed by the singing of the song, is now upon them. The repetition of all else – 'heart-wrung tears' and 'warring sighs and groans' – emphasises the ongoing emotional torment of eternal love thwarted by enforced separation.

'John Anderson, my Jo' exemplifies Burns's skill in creative assimilation. Burns took a seventeenth-century melody and varied its rhythm and intonation. He was familiar with a bawdy song with this title in which a young wife berates her aged husband for his impotence. Altering the tone and composing new words, Burns composed the song of an elderly wife reminiscing to her husband with tenderness and pride on their life together. These qualities are apparent in the first stanza where she recalls his once-black hair and unwrinkled brow. Each stanza divides into two equal parts. In stanza 1 the description of the young John Anderson contrasts with that of the man she now addresses. But the use of chiasmus ('locks...brow, brow...locks') introduces an element of patterned movement which challenges the idea of contrast, and this conveys perfectly the constancy of the love between the couple, age though they may. This is demonstrated further in the blessing which she bestows on her 'jo' or 'dear one'. In Stanza 2 the simple metaphor of life as the ascent of a hill and the careful modulation of tempo to accord with the experiences rendered combine to communicate the shared joy in both the experiences and their recollection. Mood and pace change somewhat in the last four lines, but there the continuity in the choice of metaphor – the descent of the hill leading to death – reaffirms the continuity of their love for one another.

The finest of Burns's love songs are moving statements of deep feelings. A comparable degree of commitment informs his songs on national and political themes. Burns valued the freedom of the writer to use his imaginative powers to the full, but above all he upheld the right of every individual to liberty. Following events in France with interest, Burns found much that he could endorse in the cause of the revolutionaries (for instance, he referred to the French king and queen as 'a perjured Blockhead and an un-principled Prostitute' (*Letters*, II, 334). Similarly, he sympathised with the aims underpinning the rebellion of the North American colonies and, as his 'Ode for General Washington's Birthday' indicates, regarded it as epitomising the cause of liberty.

In eighteenth-century Scotland liberty was a sensitive issue. Like many of his contemporaries, Burns had an ambivalent attitude to the Union of the Parliaments: to some extent it made commercial sense, and Burns, employed latterly by the government as an exciseman, could not be too overt in his criticism, but, on the other hand, increasing anglicisation seemed to threaten the survival of the native cultural tradition. Burns found an outlet for his nationalist sentiments in his work as collector, adapter, and writer of songs. Of these, some are overtly patriotic, and 'Scots wha hae', for instance, has become one of Scotland's alternative anthems.

Burns's finest achievement in terms of patriotic song is 'Such a Parcel of Rogues in a Nation'. This song typifies Burns's capacity for imaginative empathy. Here he speaks as an aged Scottish patriot who gives his response to the Union of 1707. It is a remarkable achievement in that Burns, casting his mind back over eighty years, is able to recreate the intense and immediate reaction of the patriotic Scot who lived through the experience of his country's uniting with England. Burns must have asked himself how such a man would have felt. His answer is to depict a complex reaction – outrage at the loss of national identity and bitterness towards those responsible. The 'Rogues' are the thirty-one Scottish Commissioners and 'parcel' is a perfect metaphor for conveying the speaker's scorn towards them in that it implies they were all packaged together for their own safety. Donald Low has drawn attention to the way in which, as with quite a number of Burns's songs, the movement of the tune dictates the arrangement of the words and clauses.[11] This is especially the case in the last four lines where the internal rhymes ('power/hour'; 'sold/gold') direct emphasis to key terms and help convey, by way of conclusion, the speaker's enforced resignation to the situation.

'A Man's a Man for a' that' (also entitled 'Is there for Honest Poverty') expresses Burns's cherished belief in the rights and the dignity of the ordinary man. Sending it to Thomson in January 1795, Burns commented,

> A great critic, Aikin on songs, says, that love and wine are the exclusive themes for song-writing. – The following is on neither subject, and consequently is no Song; but will be allowed, I think, to be two or three pretty good *prose* thoughts, inverted into rhyme (*Letters*, II, 336).

Here Burns needlessly demeans his own achievement. What he does in 'A Man's a Man for a' that' is to extend the scope of song, making it a fit medium for an affirmation of the brotherhood of man which is just as effective as that offered by Tom Paine in *The Rights of Man* (1791–2). Burns upholds the dignity and worth of honest poverty and contrasts it with the condition of the slave. The essential worth of the ordinary man is conveyed effectively by means of the metaphor of coinage. Indeed a large part of the effectiveness of this song derives from the simple but telling images and the expressive use of terms (the lord diminished by the words 'birkie' and 'cuif', for instance). In the final wish, which becomes increasingly an affirmation, internal rhymes are again used to direct emphasis to the most important terms ('pray/may'; 'worth/earth') and to suggest an inevitable movement towards universal brotherhood.

Fraternity is the key-note of 'Auld Lang Syne'. Traces of Burns's version are to be found in various earlier songs and it seems that it was the phrase itself, 'Auld lang syne', which particularly attracted Burns. On 7 December 1788 he wrote to Mrs. Dunlop,

> ...is not the Scots phrase, 'Auld lang syne', exceedingly expressive. – There is an old song and tune which have often thrilled thro' my soul. You know I am an enthusiast in old Scots songs...Light be the turf on the breast of the heaven-inspired Poet who composed this glorious Fragment! There is more of the fire of native genius in it than in half a dozen of modern English Bacchanalians (*Letters*, I, 342, 345).

It seems likely that Burns expanded and adapted the old song and, almost five years later, he sent it to Thomson with this comment:

> The air is but mediocre; but the following song, the old Song of the olden times, and which has never been in print, nor even in manuscript, untill I took it down from an old man's singing; is enough to recommend any air (*Letters*, II, 246).

The title is especially expressive and any attempt at paraphrase fails to do it justice, but it means, roughly, 'times long past' or 'times long ago'. It was essentially a drinking-song, as is evident from stanza 2, but it is much more than that. Certainly in the late eighteenth century the terms of the first stanza would evoke nostalgia for, specifically, the 'times long past' of an independent Scotland. As with so many of the finest of Burns's poems and songs, however, the most moving effect is that which develops out of individual experience. Stanzas 3 and 4 convey the speaker's recollection of shared childhood experiences. These are simply but movingly expressed:

> We twa hae run about the braes
> > And pu'd the gowans fine;
> But we've wandered mony a weary foot
> > Sin auld lang syne.

> We twa hae paidl'd i' the burn,
> > Frae mornin' sun till dine;
> But seas between us braid hae roar'd
> > Sin auld lang syne.

The pattern repeated in each of these stanzas establishes a duality of viewpoint. So meaningful were his shared childhood experiences that in recalling them the speaker virtually relives them (lines 1–2 of each stanza), but the second part of each stanza (lines 3–4) offers the present vantage-point from which he views them. Here Burns presents both what it is to be young and what it is to have been young. These stanzas, leading to the final pledge, are a celebration of a friendship that has endured, a celebration which draws its force from the evocation of the first years of the friendship and the present reaffirmation of it. It is all the more important now because, as lines 3–4 of stanzas 3 and 4 indicate, the speaker is well aware of his own mortality. The double consciousness serves as both the basis of the celebration and the means of introducing the poignant sense of aging. Here Burns affirms the value of enduring friendship but at the same time, in the speaker's awareness of being no longer young, he stresses why it is so important.

In the last six years of his life Burns devoted most of his creative energy to song. Arguably he was motivated not just by a desire to preserve part of Scotland's cultural past but also by the promptings of his own psyche. Earlier, account was taken of both Burns's immense dramatic talent and his readiness to assume the role of 'heaven-taught ploughman'. Both together and independently these factors were to create problems for him as an individual. Increasingly the most important role for Burns seems to have been that of spectator at the drama which was his own life. Added poignancy derives from the fact that he was aware of what was happening to him. In a letter in which he emphasised the importance of self-knowledge he added the wry comment, 'If to *know* one's errors were a probability of *mending* them, I stand a fair chance' (*Letters*, I, 60). Ever more self-absorbed, Burns seems to have become a prisoner of the personae that he assumed. His letters reveal a sense of having to live up (or sometimes down) to the various parts which he could so readily play. This comment in a letter to Ainslie says much:

> There is one thing for which I set great store by you as a friend, and it is this, that I have not a friend upon earth, besides yourself, to whom I can talk nonsense without forfeiting some degree of his esteem (*Letters*, I, 129).

Though a person of great wit and charm, Burns appears from a number of his letters to have suffered from both acute depression and a sense of alienation. He writes variously of 'gloomy conjectures in the dark vista of Futurity' (*Letters*, I, 305); ' my hell within, and all around me' (*Letters*, II, 121); and 'this disparity between our wishes and our powers' (*Letters*, II, 202); and in another letter he notes, 'my nerves are in a damnable State' (*Letters*, II, 3). In this context probably the most revealing passage of all is that in which he entreats Erskine of Mar to burn the letter he has just received because

> BURNS, in whose behalf you have so generously interested yourself, I have here, in his native colours, drawn *as he is*; but should any of the people in whose hands is the very bread he eats, get the least knowledge of the picture, it would ruin the poor Bard for ever (*Letters*, II, 210).

Burns's stylistic virtuosity is both a symptom of, and a compensation for, the acute sense of displacement which he experienced. It may well be that his function as song-collector gave him some respite from the troubling questions of identity. His collecting and adapting of songs may well have given direction and coherence to his life. Indeed, that synthesizing activity may well have served as a means of synthesizing or re-integrating some of the disparate selves of the poet. Arguably Burns found an identity in precisely that function wherein he collected, revised, and stabilised such an important part of his country's cultural tradition.

REFERENCES

1. Robert Burns, *Letters*, ed J. De Lancey Ferguson, 2nd edn, ed. G. Ross Roy, (Oxford, 1985), I, 15.
2. Robert Burns's *Commonplace Book 1783–1785*, introduced by David Daiches (London, 1965), 1.
3. Thomas Crawford, *Burns: A Study of the Poems and Songs* (Edinburgh, 1965), 104.
4. Donald Low (ed), *Burns: The Critical Heritage* (London and Boston, 1974), 102.
5. William Wallace, *The Life and Works of Robert Burns*, ed. R. Chambers, 4 vols. (Edinburgh and London, 1896), I, 68–9.
6. David Daiches, *Robert Burns* (2nd edn; reptd Edinburgh, 1981), 153.
7. James Mackay, *Burns: A Biography of Robert Burns* (Edinburgh, 1992), 170.
8. William Montgomerie, *New Judgements on Robert Burns* (Glasgow, 1947), 79–83.
9. Lionel Trilling, *Beyond Culture* (Harmondsworth, 1967), 54.
10. John Ashmead and John Davison, 'Words, Music and Emotion in the Love Songs of Robert Burns', *Sociability and Society in Eighteenth-Century Scotland*, ed. John Dwyer and Richard B. Sher (Edinburgh, 1993), 237.
11. Donald A. Low, *Robert Burns* (Edinburgh, 1986), 127.

BIBLIOGRAPHY

Editions

Poems and Songs of Robert Burns, edited and introduced by
James Barke (London and Glasgow: Collins, 1955).
The Poems and Songs of Robert Burns, edited by James Kinsley
(Oxford: Clarendon Press, 1968).
The Letters of Robert Burns, edited by J. De Lancey Ferguson;
second edition edited by G. Ross Roy (Oxford: Clarendon Press,
1985).

Criticism and Biography

John Ashmead and John Davison, 'Works, Music and Emotion in
the Love Songs of Robert Burns', *Sociability and Society in
Eighteenth-Century Scotland,* ed. John Dwyer and Richard B.
Sher (Edinburgh: Mercat Press, 1993).
Thomas Crawford, *Burns: A Study of the Poems and Songs*
(Edinburgh: Oliver and Boyd, 1960; second edn., 1965).
David Daiches, *Robert Burns* (Revised edn., 1966; reptd
Edinburgh: Spurbooks, 1981).
R. D. S. Jack and Andrew Noble (eds.) *The Art of Robert Burns*
(London: Vision Press, 1982).
Donald A. Low (ed.), *Robert Burns: The Critical Heritage* (London:
Routledge, 1974).
Donald A. Low (ed.), *Critical Essays on Robert Burns* (London:
Routledge, 1975).
Donald A. Low (ed.), *Robert Burns* (Edinburgh: Scottish Academic
Press, 1986).
Donald A. Low (ed.), *The Songs of Robert Burns* (London:
Routledge, 1993).
Carol McGuirk, *Robert Burns and the Sentimental Era* (Athens,
Georgia: University of Georgia Press, 1985)
James Mackay, *Burns: A Biography of Robert Burns* (Edinburgh:
Mainstream, 1992).
Kenneth Simpson, *The Protean Scot: The Crisis of Identity in
Eighteenth-Century Scottish Literature* (Aberdeen: Aberdeen
University Press, 1988).
Kenneth Simpson (ed.), *Burns Now* (Edinburgh: Canongate,
1994).

Study Aids

John Hodgart, *Robert Burns: Study Guide for Revised Higher* (ASLS, 1993).

R. D. S. Jack, *Three Poems of Burns* ('Tam O' Shanter', 'John Anderson, my Jo', and 'Holly Willie's Prayer') (ASLS Commentary-Cassette No 7).

Mairi Robinson (ed.), *The Concise Scots Dictionary* (Aberdeen: Aberdeen University Press, 1985).

INDEX OF POEMS AND SONGS

Poems and songs which are the subject of detailed commentary are marked with an asterisk.

80

TEACHING AIDS

ASLS Commentary Cassettes

The following audio cassette commentaries have been produced
and are now available:

Hogg's *Confessions of a Justified Sinner*
Douglas Gifford   (£5.00)

Fourteen Poems of Sorley Maclean
Iain Crichton Smith (with readings from Sorley Maclean) (£5.00)

Seventeen Poems of Edwin Morgan
Roderick Watson (with readings from Edwin Morgan)   (£5.00)

Nineteen Poems of Norman MacCaig
Edwin Morgan (with readings from Norman MacCaig)   (£5.00)

Eleven Poems of Edwin Muir
Margery McCulloch (with readings from Roderick Watson) (£5.00)

Cloud Howe and Grey Granite
Ian Campbell with readings from Arthur Stewart   (£5.00)

The following cassettes are available to schools and members only

Sunset Song
Douglas Young   (£3.50)

The House with the Green Shutters (A) Tone
Ian Campbell   (£3.50)

The House with the Green Shutters (B) Characterisation
Ian Campbell   (£3.50)

The Silver Darlings
Douglas Young   (£3.50)

Three Poems of Burns
R. D. S. Jack ('Tam O' Shanter', 'John Anderson, my Jo',
'Holy Willie's prayer')   (£3.50)

R. L. Stevenson's 'Thrawn Janet' and 'Markheim'
Ian Campbell   (£3.50)

Two Short Stories of Carl MacDougall
Elaine Petrie (with readings from Carl MacDougall)   (£3.50)

Fifteen Poems of Iain Crichton Smith
John Blackburn (with readings from Iain Crichton Smith) (£3.50)

Spartacus
Ian Campbell   (£3.50)

SCOTNOTES

Study guides to major Scottish writers and literary texts

Produced by the Schools and Further Education Committee
of the Association for Scottish Literary Studies

Series Editors
Lorna Borrowman Smith
Ronald Renton

Editorial Board

THE ASSOCIATION FOR SCOTTISH LITERARY STUDIES
aims to promote the study, teaching and writing of Scottish
literature, and to further the study of the languages of
Scotland.

To these ends, the ASLS publishes works of Scottish literature;
literary criticism and in-depth reviews of Scottish books in
Scottish Studies Review; short articles, features and news in
ScotLit; and scholarly studies of language in *Scottish
Language*. It also publishes *New Writing Scotland*, an annual
anthology of new poetry, drama and short fiction, in Scots,
English and Gaelic. ASLS has also prepared a range of
teaching materials covering Scottish language and literature
for use in schools.

All the above publications are available in return for an annual
subscription. Schools can receive teaching materials by joining
ASLS at a special reduced rate. Enquiries should be sent to:

ASLS, c/o Department of Scottish History, 9 University
Gardens, University of Glasgow, Glasgow G12 8QH.

Telephone/fax +44 (0)141 330 5309
e-mail d.jones@asls.org.uk
www.asls.org.uk